GENEALOGY

of the

LORD FAMILY

WHICH REMOVED FROM
COLCHESTER, CONNECTICUT, TO HANOVER,
NEW HAMPSHIRE, AND THEN TO NORWICH, VERMONT

Reverend John M. Lord

HERITAGE BOOKS
2014

HERITAGE BOOKS

AN IMPRINT OF HERITAGE BOOKS, INC.

Books, CDs, and more—Worldwide

For our listing of thousands of titles see our website
at
www.HeritageBooks.com

A Facsimile Reprint
Published 2014 by
HERITAGE BOOKS, INC.
Publishing Division
5810 Ruatan Street
Berwyn Heights, Md. 20740

1

Originally published
Concord, New Hampshire:
Ira C. Evans Co., Printers
1903

Prefactory Note

The numerals I, II, III, IV, etc. are used to
designate the generation of the individual.

The figures (1), (5), (7), (12), (20), etc.,
are used for reference.

International Standard Book Numbers
Paperbound: 978-0-7884-1186-1
Clothbound: 978-0-7884-6060-9

THE LORD FAMILY.

Sailed from England, in the ship "Elisabeth and Ann," Roger Cooper, master, April 29, 1635, Thomas Lord and Dorothy his wife, taking with them seven children whose names were as follows: Thomas, Ann, William, John, Robert, Amie [Aymie] and Dorothy, the eldest being sixteen and the youngest four years old. Thomas Lord at this date was fifty, and his wife forty-six. It would be easy to show that he was a man of means, of position, and of influence, but this is not the place to do it. He came from Essex county, Eng., which is to the north and east of London, and one account says from Weathersfield in that county. His ancestor is said to be John Lord; whether this means father or more remote ancestor is not known.

They landed at Boston and lived one year in Cambridge; the next year, 1636, in a company of a hundred, with whom went the famous Rev. Dr. Hooker and an associate, they removed by land through the wilderness to Hartford, Conn., where he was at the division of lands in 1639. He is the ancestor of all the Lords in Connecticut, and of those who have removed from it.

Of his children, the eldest appears to be Richard, six or eight years, it may be, older than any of those already mentioned, and who seems to have come to America some years before his father, for he is found in Hingham or Braintree, Mass., or in both, but who after his father's removal to Hartford, Conn., followed him there, for he is found in 1642 as the constable of the town. He afterwards settled in New London, Conn., where he became a very prominent citizen, as a military man, and then as a ship owner in the carrying trade between that port and the West Indies, and where his grave is found at this day.

Thomas, the second son, became the first physician and surgeon of Hartford, but he afterwards settled as physician in Weathersfield, where he died. His third son, William, settled in Old Saybrook at the mouth of the Connecticut river, where he died in 1678. He had a large family of sons: The eldest, William, born 1643; died in 1696; settled in Haddam, doubtless in that part now called East Haddam. He married Mary Shaler, who after his decease married Samuel Ingraham. He left a family of eight children: Mary, born 1678; William, born 1680; Sarah, born 1682; Jonathan, born 1685; Nathaniel, born 1687; Hannah, born 1689; John, born 1693; Dorothy, a child of nine months.

Of two of the sons in this family the writer knows nothing, except that one author says William, the eldest, died in 1736, aged fifty-six, apparently in East Haddam, having lived possibly on his father's farm, and leaving a widow; the same writer says Nathaniel died in 1740, apparently in East Haddam, he also leaving a widow.

Robert Lord settled at Ipswich, Mass., and was the ancestor of Judge Otis B. Lord, of Salem, Mass.; of Henry D. Lord, of Boston, Mass., the genealogist of the Lords in and around Athol, Mass., and of some who went up into Vermont and settled in Brattleboro and other towns to the north.

Nathaniel, or Nathan, Lord settled at Kittery, Me., and was the ancestor of the Lords in Maine, and of those who came into New Hampshire from Berwick, Me., and vicinity.

The question has arisen: " Were these two Lords related to Thomas Lord of Hartford, Conn.?" " Family Tradition " says they were brothers; but one who has given much attention to this matter finds no confirmation of this statement, yet concludes that they were relatives, and probably cousins.

We come now to THE PROBLEM *of this genealogy:* It was this: *Was that Mr. Lord of Colchester, Conn.,* the ancestor of the Lords of Hanover, N. H., and Norwich, Vt., *the son of this William Lord of Haddam, or of some other man? What was his name? And where was he born?* This problem has caused the writer much trouble and perplexity. On the one side are these things, facts of one kind : Neither Mr. Lord of Colchester, nor his son who died in Norwich, Vt., left any records as such (for years this was supposed to be literally true) to show what his real name was, who his father was, or where he was born; nor did they make any such verbal statements as to fill the minds and be retained in the memory of their descendants; on the contrary it came to be believed as a positive fact by two generations, grandsons and great grandsons of this ancestor, those too with whom his son, their father and grandfather, died, that *his name was Jonathan* and it was *so written down* in the family Bible of a grandson, among the Family Records— *Jonathan Lord of Colchester, Conn.*—furthermore, they said he came directly from England to Colchester, Conn. But all these statements and beliefs have proved to be entirely erroneous, yet so confidently were they made, that the writer could not for a long time indulge the thought that his ancestor's name could be any other than "*Jonathan.*"

The proof in the case is of different kinds, and from several different sources. One part of it is this: One author says, "Jonathan Lord, son of this William of Haddam, went to Colchester, and then was lost sight of"; and it was thought that he had been found in the person of the writer's grandfather's grandfather, Jonathan Lord; but a later "History of Sharon," in the western part of Connecticut, says, "Jonathan Lord of Colchester came to Sharon, with his son Joseph, as one of the first settlers in 1743, and died there in 1760." This seems to dispose of Jonathan, the son of William of Haddam, and also of *Jonathan* as *the name* of my ancestor. Again, this same author says, "John, the son of this William Lord, went to Hebron, Conn., and died there in 1746," but an examination of the town records of Hebron, finds no mention of any John Lord before or after that date; this if not faulty shows that this John Lord could not have lived there, and must be looked for elsewhere.

We come now to the *positive proof* (from documents recently found) that this ancestor's name *was John*, that his native place was East Haddam, and that without a doubt he was the son of this William. The first proof is from a deed of land. Deacon Thomas Skinner of Colchester, county of Hartford, Conn., " in consideration of twenty and four pounds," conveyed to *"John Lord of East Haddam,"* in same county, " fifty acres of land, which is my fourth division of land in the township of Colchester aforesaid, to take up, lay out, and record for himself the said fifty acres " (of wild land) ; and this was done " the twenty-fourth of January, 1717-'18." This deed is in the writer's hands, and was brought to Norwich, Vt., by this John Lord's son.

Here are three things shown : One is, his name was John ; the second, his home, residence, or native place was East Haddam, and then, if he was the son of Wil liam Lord, his age would be twenty-four or twenty-five years. The second proof is from the town records of Colchester. These state that *"John Lord"* married a first and second wife, both being from East Haddam, and one of these women is known to be the mother of the man who came from Colchester, Conn., to Norwich, Vt. The third proof is from the will, which I will give entire.

" In the name of God, Amen. I *John Lord*, of Colchester, in the County of Hartford, and Colony of Connecticut in New England, being under difficulty of body, but of perfect mind and memory,—Thanks be given to God for it!—calling to mind my own mortality, and knowing that it is appointed for all men once to die, do make this my last Will and Testament. As touching such worldly things wherewith God has blessed me in this life, I give, demise, and dispose of the same in mode and form as follows : Item, I give to my son John one shilling lawful money; Item, I give to my daughter Sarah two pounds lawful money; all the rest I give to [my] son Jonathan, he paying Sarah and maintaining me and his mother so long as she shall continue my widow. In testimony hereof I have hereunto set my hand and seal.

"Dated in Colchester, February the 28th, 1759. 'John Lord.'"

The writing and the signing of the above will appears to have been done by the same hand and pen. And this will the son of the testator brought to Norwich, Vt.

Now then, considering the name, the native place, and the age—considering also that no other John Lord has been found to fill the vacant place—the conclusion seems satisfactory that John Lord of Colchester, Conn., was the son of William Lord of Haddam. And thus the lost link of connection with ancestors is found and established.

Having purchased in January fifty acres of wild land, he began to clear it, and the next year apparently he built a house, for at the close of it he brought there a wife to make for him a home; here his children were born and grew up, and here he lived for more than forty years. This home was in what was called " Pine Swamp " Society, but is now the parish of " West Chester," in the town of Colchester. John Lord of Colchester married Hannah Ackley of East Haddam; she having died, he married Experience Crippen, daughter of Thomas Crippen of East Haddam, and sister of Jabez Crippen of Colchester, who afterwards went to Sharon, Conn., and then removed to Manchester, Vt., where he died. The town records give also the marriage of two or three of his other sisters in Colchester. This family of Crippens would seem to have been Scotch-Irish, of good blood, and lately come over from the old country; all of these particulars would fill out the family tradition relative to this Experience Crippen. (See now the town records.)

I. (1) John Lord of Colchester, Conn. (son of William of East Haddam, son of William of Saybrook, son of Thomas of Hartford), b. East Haddam, 1693; d. Bolton, Conn., Sept. (probably), 1761; m. (1st) Hannah Ackley of East Haddam, Dec. 25, 1718.

CHILDREN.

II. (2) Sarah, b. April 7, 1721.

(3) John, b. March 3, 1722.

Of this Sarah and this John Lord, nothing further is known, except that they were living in 1759, as mentioned in the will as given above.

He m. (2d) Experience Crippen of East Haddam,
Dec. 26, 1754.

II. (4) Jonathan, b. [Old Style] Oct. 3, 1726; or as it is in
Family Records [New Style] Oct. 14, 1725; d.
Norwich, Vt., May 8, 1805; m. Ruth Rogers of
Colchester, Conn., Nov. 20, 1746.

Ruth Rogers was born July 21, 1725; died in Norwich, Vt., August 27, 1808; she was born probably in Harwich, Mass., as her father, Nathaniel, lived there that year. He was the youngest son of John Rogers and Elizabeth Twining, of that part of Eastham, Mass., now called Orleans; he, Nathaniel, married two wives, and the mother of Ruth—Silence Dimmock—was the second wife; Ruth had two half sisters, one own brother—Nehemiah—older, and two brothers—Jabes and Nathaniel—younger than herself, also three sisters younger than she.

She was *the fifth* in descent from Thomas Rogers of Plymouth, Mass., in the following line: Thomas, Joseph, John, Nathaniel and Ruth. This Thomas Rogers came over in " The Mayflower," and was one of those who signed the compact in her cabin, but with others died that first sad winter, leaving in Plymouth his oldest son Joseph, who came over with him. It would seem that his wife had died in England. In the spring of 1621, those of the pilgrims who were left were divided into companies of thirteen, to whom allotments of land were made; one company, including Governor

Bradford and family, also Joseph Rogers received an allotment south of Plymouth village on the east side of the road leading to Sandwich. Writing in 1650, Governor Bradford familiarly says: "Thomas Rogers died in the first sickness, but his son is still living and is married and hath six children, the rest of his children came over and are married and have many children," showing that Thomas Rogers' other sons came over later. One authority would have it that Joseph's children were born in Plymouth and Duxbury, while another says they were all born in Sandwich. Some of them may have been born in Plymouth, but all were baptized in Sandwich. Perhaps those born in Plymouth and Duxbury were the children of Joseph's brothers. The names of Joseph's children were these: Sarah—died in infancy—Joseph, Thomas, Eliza, John, Mary, and Hannah. Joseph Rogers, after living a longer or shorter time in Sandwich, removed in 1655 to Eastham, Mass., where he died in 1678. His son John was the executor of his will, as said above. This John was the father of Nathaniel, the father of Ruth, the wife of Jonathan Lord. This is all plain so far in the line of descent.

This Ruth Lord was a woman of excellent common sense, of clear perception, shrewd and sound in judgment, and to the last of her life constantly affirmed that she was *the seventh* in descent from *John Rogers*, the martyr who was burned at Smithfield, Eng., Feb. 14, 1555. If she was correct in this, Thomas Rogers of " The Mayflower" was the grandson of the martyr.

About *the matter of descent* this may be said in
general : Those were times when family registers were
not kept, as they are now, but what is contained in
them was handed down from father to son and by
mother to daughter; it was the family tradition, but
back of it was *a glorious fact*, embodied in it but not
built on myth or foolish pride.

There are many families in New England who trace
their lineage from Rev. John Rogers, for many years a
noted minister of Dedham, Eng., and through him to
Rev. John Rogers, the martyr.

Now, what are the facts? Rev. John Rogers of
Dedham, Eng., their ancestor, was the son of John
Rogers of Chelmsford, Essex county, Eng., east of
London, while John Rogers, the martyr, was the son
of John Rogers of Deritend—now a part of Birming-
ham—county of Warwick, and northwest of London.
This shows that John Rogers of Dedham, Eng., though
a descendant of one John Rogers, could not be a
descendant of John Rogers the martyr. This is one
part of the facts, and to a certain extent negative ; the
other part is as follows : The children of the martyr
were these eleven, Daniel, John, Ambrose, Samuel,
Phillip, Bernard, Augustine, Barnaby, Susan, Elisabeth
and Hester ; and the children of Daniel, the eldest son,
were Daniel, William, Edward, Ellen and Joan ; and
the children of John, the second son, were Cassandra,
Elisabeth, Hecuba, Constantine, John, Edward, Mary
and Varro (a son). Among these grandchildren of
the martyr appears no Thomas; but there remain six

other sons who may have left children, and among them may have been a Thomas; nothing is now known to prove or disprove this; it may be, or may not be, shown in the future that Thomas Rogers of "The Mayflower" was the son of *one of these six sons* of the martyr.

CHILDREN OF JONATHAN AND RUTH LORD.

III. (5) Nathaniel, b. Colchester, Conn., Dec. 25, 1747, d. Hanover, N. H., Sept. 25, 1837. (He was named from his mother's father.)
(6) Experience, b. Colchester, Conn., Feb. 14, 1750; d. in Craftsbury, Vt., 1822. (Named from the father's mother.)
(7) Jonathan, b. Colchester, Conn., Feb. 17, 1752; d. Norwich, Vt., Feb. 27, 1821. (Named from his father.)
(8) Ruth, b. Colchester, Conn., May 12, 1754; d. Norwich, Vt., March 3, 1838. (Named for her mother)
(9) David, b. Colchester, Conn., Aug. 4, 1756; d. Norwich, Vt., Jan. 25, 1803 or 1804.
(10) John, b., probably, in Colchester, Conn., date unknown and d. in childhood.
(11) Ichabod, b. Bolton, Conn., April 7, 1763; d. in Shalersville, Portage Co., Ohio, May 16, 1852.
(12) Joseph, b. Bolton, Conn., May 4, 1764; d. near Jamestown, Green Co., Ohio, August, 1847.

John Lord of Colchester *wrote* his will apparently the twentieth of February, 1759, though it was not *signed* till the twenty-eighth, giving substantially all his property to his son Jonathan, being now about thirty-four years old. This son went immediately to Bolton, Conn., and bought up a farm there; for John Hills of this town, February 21, gave him a deed of 140 acres of land for "400 pounds lawful money," already paid to this John Hills. Bolton at this time included what is now Bolton and the township of Vernon, lying north of it; this Vernon on the west joins onto (East) Windsor. This farm of one hundred and forty acres lay in the western part of Vernon; the highway running north and south, nearest to Windsor was its eastern boundary; the farm of Benjamin Talcott was on the south, and the township line of (East) Windsor was its western boundary. The farm must have had a good location, not far from the present village of Talcottville. Onto this farm Jonathan Lord doubtless moved the same year, taking with him his father (and his mother); and here in 1761 his father died, apparently in September, for his will was presented for probate September 17, 1761, and what is more definite as to the place is this: Certain men were appointed to appraise his personal property; they give a list of the articles—all old and worn—with the appraised value of each; the sum of these values foots up and gives 16 lbs. 15 shillings and 3 pence, but what is more important the heading of this list reads thus: "Bolton, *Oct. 2, 1761.* We, the subscribers, being appointed and under oath to prize the estate of John Lord, late of Bolton, deceased." Having purchased and occupied this valuable farm, why, now, did not this Jonathan Lord continue to live here and enjoy his home here? The family tradition tells us why: Being "bound" for a man, he had to pay the bond, losing so much as the result, he had to lease his farm and then, with what he could save from the wreck, make for himself a new home elsewhere. This new home was made in Hanover, N. H.

The history of the family for a few years is partly documentary and partly family tradition. The History of Hanover, as a town, says that Mr. Edmund Freeman was *the first settler in town*, coming from Mansfield, Conn., in 1765, and his wife was the first *white* woman to winter in it; also that Mr. Jonathan Curtice, having begun a settlement the same summer, brought his family the next spring. The family tradition comes from three different branches of it. One part is this: The man with whom Jonathan Lord and wife lived for twenty-five years, and with whom they died, gave the writer forty years ago the date of 1763 as the year when they removed to Hanover, N. H.; this manifestly is an error as to the time of their coming, but may be true of the year when the farm in Bolton, Conn., was sold and when they decided to go to Hanover, the time when they began to lay their plans and direct all their efforts to this end. Tradition in the family makes great account of *the year 1763*, and this I interpret as true of the time when the farm was sold, when the decision was made to make the next home in Hanover, and when Jonathan Lord came up there to make a pitch or selection of land on which to settle; also that same year a son was born, and the name given him—Ichabod—*may* have had its occasion or origin in the loss of the farm.

Another part is this: The tradition in the family of their eldest son says that Mr. Freeman's family was *the first* to come to Hanover, and his father's *the second*, also that the family came when he was eighteen years old, 1766; likewise that the father and eldest son came up the previous summer, cleared land, erected a log house, and in the autumn returned to Connecticut.

Part third says their daughter Ruth came up the Connecticut river when she was eleven years old, 1765, and that her coming was with a woman who was the first to winter in Hanover; this she used to tell over and over to her children; now she was, as has been said, eleven years old in 1765.

But all these facts and statements can be harmonized in this way, and the following is given as probably the true account:

In the summer of 1765 the father and the eldest son, Nathaniel, came up to Hanover—came in all probability in company with Mr. Freeman, his family and Mr. Curtice, the second daughter, Ruth, coming with Mrs. Freeman; thus there would be three men and a lad of seventeen years to assist each other in building their three log houses, and in any other work that required assistance. During the summer and early autumn they cleared land, erected a log house, and, presumably, also sowed some winter grain; then later in the autumn they returned to Connecticut, leaving the daughter Ruth with Mrs. Freeman. Early the next spring, 1766, the father, the mother, and the younger children—the youngest, Joseph, being yet a babe not two years old, and carried in his mother's arms—came up the Connecticut river in a pine canoe ; these two things, *the babe carried in his mother's arms* and *the pine canoe* are assured *facts ;* they came up *earlier* in the spring than the Curtice family, and so came *ahead* of them ; while the three or four older children came up by land in an ox cart—if there was a cart—as far at least as Charlestown ; and so this was *the second family* that came into the township of Hanover.

John Wright was one of the original proprietors of this township ; his claim included the lot, a part of which is *the common* at Hanover Center ; the lot next west from this in the east and west range was assigned to the " Society for Propagating the Gospel," while directly south from this lot in north and south range was the " Globe Lot." It is probable, nay it is morally certain, that Jonathan Lord made his settlement on the lot belonging to the " Gospel Propagation Society " ; and this explains what was for a long time a very perplexing thing : First, why his name did not appear among those of the " proprietors," or early owners of land in the township ; and second, the absence for several years of his name from the list of taxpayers to the town ; instead of paying taxes to the town he paid rent to the " Gospel Propagation Society." This " Lot " was composed largely of a great hill and has to this day been called " Lord's Hill."

The following occurrence is said by one of the parties concerned in it to have happened while they had their home on this " Hill." One winter's day the father and his eldest son went down west to the river on some business, and having finished this started on their return home. The day had been bitterly cold, and as it drew to its close the cold increased in severity. Their path or road undoubtedly was substantially the same as the road now leading up from the river around over the northwest shoulder of the " Hill," where is now the Spencer place, then directly east along the north end of the " Hill," past the residence of Deacon Fellows on to the " Old Center." When they had come nearly to the Fellows' place, their path would turn directly south up the remaining ascent to their home. Having gone part of this distance, the son complained of the cold and a very great drowsiness, and wished to lie down; but the father cut a switch, and applied it so vigorously to the son that his drowsiness soon left him, and his blood so tingled in his veins that he was ready to go again on their way homeward. However, they had gone but part of this distance when the father complained of the cold and this same drowsiness, and himself wished to lie down and rest; then the son got a switch and applied it to the father with such earnestness that his drowsiness left him, and he was ready to go on their way. They reached their home in safety, both father and son, having been saved from death as *the result* of a *good whipping*.

All the early settlers of that day, if they were not pinched with poverty, suffered many privations incident to the life of settlers, and the Lords suffered with them. The following is true of them while they had their home on the " Hill," or at a later date while living elsewhere : many a time their only meal was roasted potatoes, without salt, and ashes sprinkled on in place of pepper, eaten, too—it may be—in the chimney corner. Their home continued some three years here on this " Hill." In the mean time, not finding the soil of the farm he was on so good as he had expected, he made arrangements for a home elsewhere. For in " December, 1769, Jonathan Lord bought for thirteen pounds of David Richardson, of Somers, Conn., one of the original grantees of the township of Hanover, N. H., three lots of land, they being all his right, title or interest in the town of Hanover." The first of these was the " Town Lot" (this was one division of the " Original Town Center," as laid out by the proprietors, but never built upon or occupied by anybody), the next was a River " Lott," and the third a lot yet unsurveyed. Evidently it was this third lot lying some half a mile south of the common, on which he built a house and where he lived for a time. It is in the location of these two homes that we have the satisfying or fulfilling of the old family tradition, that " they lived west and south of the old cemetery on the common at Hanover Center." The old meeting-house at the Center used to stand at the south end of the common and the cemetery was to the west or southwest of this; the home on the hill, west of the cemetery, meets the first condition of the tradition, and the second home on the south road satisfies the second condition.

In 1770 or 1771 he sold this farm or exchanged for land elsewhere. One family narrative says: "He exchanged his farm at the Center with a man (named Hatch it is thought),who afterwards built on it a large two-story wood house on the east side of the road, and east of the little brook running between it and the road. This house is standing now and is occupied, or was quite recently, by a man whose name is Monahan.

Jonathan Lord moved down onto the bank of the Connecticut river, and lived in a house that stood on the rise of ground just north of the little brook that comes in at the old ferry; this ferry is immediately north of the Timothy Smith farm (now the Franklin Smith), Hanover; the road to the ferry went through the field immediately adjoining Mr. Smith's house. Himself or his son David had the care of this ferry more or less of the time they lived in Hanover.

In 1770, November 8, "Jonathan Lord, of Hanover, N. H., deeded to his son Nathaniel for twenty pounds the one hundred acre lot he had recently bought of David Richardson." September 21, 1772, Nathaniel Lord bought of Isaac Bridgeman of Hanover, N. H., three "river lots," so called, on the bank of the Connecticut river, for seventy pounds. These constituted the farm on which Nathaniel Lord lived and died, his son Isaac W. lived and died, and which is now the home of his daughter Rhoda W., the wife of Simeon C. Field.

In 1772, April 20, John Wright of Hanover, N. H., deeded to "Jonathan Lord of Hanover," one hundred acres of land in Norwich, Vt., for thirty-five pounds.

This deed not having been recorded, the sale possibly fell through, though the money appears to have been paid, and the deed certainly was witnessed and given.

In 1773, September 28, John Shafter of Norwich, Vt., gave a deed to " Jonathan Lord of *Hanover, N. H.*," of " five rights " of land lying on both sides of the Ompompanoosuc river, and in Norwich, Vt., for forty pounds; as this land was that on which he and his son David lived and where both of them died, it would appear that this Jonathan Lord did not remove into Norwich, Vt., until the autumn of 1773, and still further, this " Jonathan Lord *of Norwich, Vt.*," bound himself to give before January 1, 1774, a deed to this same John Shafter of two or three lots of land in Hanover, and which Jonathan Lord had obtained from this David Richardson; thus disposing of all the Richardson land, and also showing that *he had removed into Norwich, Vt.*, before the beginning of of 1774, having come probably in the latter part of September or early in October.

On the meadow west of the Ompompanoosuc, on land once owned by John Shafter, Jonathan Lord and David, his son, built a log house the location of which is still seen by the hollow remaining from the cellar. This meadow is now owned and occupied by the daughters of Asa Lord, the son of David. In this house Jonathan Lord lived until his son David had built a frame house on the hill east of the river, where he lived with that son, till he died before his father, and where he died, and his wife after him.

Sometimes while living in that house on the meadow, which became at length a house of plenty, their larder became low in variety at least if not in quantity; on one of these occasions, in the spring the men found a large *salmon fish* stranded on a sand bar in the river; they carried it up to the house for food, and the report of it said: "I tell you, it was *proper good eating*."

The occasion of his settling in *Norwich, Vt.*, may have been this: John Rogers, a relative of his wife, had come to Norwich, bought a farm of fifty acres— more or less—on the west side of the Ompompanoosuc, and adjoining the land of James Waterman to the south of it, the larger part of which farm is now owned by Joseph H. Cloud; on the meadow near the bank of the river, he built a log house, the soil by its color still showing where it stood; in this house he lived till he had built, on the west side of the road then running north and south through the town, the first frame house erected in that part of the town, or in that part now in the neighborhood of Union Village; this house, afterwards changed and enlarged, was the one in which the writer was born. Mr. Rogers at a later date sold this farm to a man by the name of Barrett, and removed into Thetford, Vt., on the south road leading up to the "Hill," lived and died in a house standing on land now owned by Charles C. Senter. This Mr. Rogers seems to have invited his relative to come from Hanover, N. H., and buy of John Shafter the land adjoining his own on the south and east, all this Jonathan Lord certainly did.

Another result of John Rogers' coming to Norwich, Vt., was this: Four years after Jonathan Lord bought his farm in Norwich, Vt., this Jonathan Lord's son Jonathan came down from Strafford, Vt., and bought the fifty acres next north of John Rogers' land, thus bringing a circle of relatives together into this one neighborhood.

Their methods of traveling in those early days may interest somewhat: In 1766 Jonathan Lord moved a part of his family up the Connecticut river in a pine canoe, the mother bringing her youngest child—then a babe—in her arms. This was one method, up and down the Connecticut river, their greatest thoroughfare, in *a canoe* for several years. Six or seven years later, while David Lord, then living on the bank of the Connecticut, was preparing to take a load of turnips over the river (possibly these vegetables were intended to be used in their new home in Norwich, Vt.), a man and his daughter came up desiring to be ferried across the river; they had ridden all the way on horseback from Mansfield, Conn. (she doubtless on a pillion behind her father). This was the first meeting of two young people who never once dreamed that day that some years later they should be husband and wife. This was a second method of traveling, *on horseback*, men and women, up and down the country for hundreds of miles.

In 1762 the proprietors of the township of Hanover voted to build a road from Charlestown (No. 4) to and through Hanover. In 1764 a committee appointed by them reported on the expense already incurred by a community of the four towns, Hanover, Norwich, Lebanon and Hartford, in building this road; they allowed and ordered to be paid by Hanover sixteen and one half pounds. In October of this year this road was laid out and cleared, i. e., of brush, trees and stumps. In 1767 other roads were completed. Till a grist-mill was built in town, about 1777, everybody carried their grain to Charlestown.

Nathaniel Lord, son of Jonathan, used to tell his children that, after he had a home of his own, he for years used to carry his grain to get it ground down to Charlestown, N. H. If in the summer, then of course it was carried in a canoe; but probably this was chiefly done in the winter, and if so, on the ice, so in the winter they went up and down the river *on the ice.*

Doubtless they had oxen, as at a later date, to do their work on the farm; but up to this time it does not appear that there were any such roads in town, or through the several towns, that oxen and carts could travel on them.

Another thing showing the difference between those times and the present was this: It used to be said that whatever family, in those days, " had a *barrel of potatoes* " thought they had a " *large supply for a whole year.* "

Nathaniel Lord mentioned above, and the same is true of his brother Jonathan, was one of the " one hundred *minute men,*" who were called out by Colonel House of Hanover, N. H., (this man lived next south of where Franklin Smith lives, and on the farm now owned by Mr. William Fullington,) to repel the Indians in their attack on Royalton, Vt. During his absence from home, Mrs. Nathaniel Lord, in that time of terror and alarm, had for her aid and comfort her husband's younger brother, Ichabod. Mr. Jonathan Lord was living then where neighbors were comparatively near, and so his wife did not need any one in a special manner to give her cheer or protection.

LORD.

III. (5) Nathaniel Lord married Lois Copp, 1775. She was born in Concord, N. H., April 18, 1757; died in Hanover, N. H., February 27, 1841.

CHILDREN.

IV. (13) Sarah, b. and d. not given.
(14) Rebecca, d. aged about 20.
(15) Rhoda, d. aged 18 or 19.
(16) Isaac, d. in infancy.
(17) Isaac Walbridge, b. May 8, 1790; d. Aug. 22, 1864.
(18) Jonathan, b. Mar. 1795; d. Westville, N. Y., Sept. 1, 1883.

STOWELL.

IV. (13) Sarah Lord married, date unknown, Ira Stowell of Thetford, Vt.

CHILDREN.

V. (19) Elam Nathaniel, b. and d. unknown.
(20) Ira, b. and d. unknown.
(21) Sarah, b. not given; d. aged 13 or 14.

LORD.

IV. (17) Isaac W. Lord married Lucy Brown of Hanover Center, January 1, 1811. She was born April 25, 1792; died December 17, 1831.

CHILDREN.

V. (22) Amanda Rebecca, b. Oct. 9, 1811.
(23) Harvey Brown, b. Sept. 23, 1813; d. not given.
(24) Rhoda Walbridge, b. Jan. 23, 1816.
(25) Tryphena Evaline, d. at age of eight months.
(26) Lucy Lavina, d. three months old.
(27) Mary Lavina, b. Aug. 7, year not given.
(28) Elisabeth Ann Davis, b. Apr. 23, 1828; d. Jan. 16, 1832.

IV. (17) Isaac W. Lord married (second time) Thankful Tilden of Lebanon, N. H., February 14, 1832.

COPP.

V. (22) Amanda Rebecca Lord married April 14, 1832, Charles Copp of Sanbornton, N. H. Their present home is Newburyport, Mass.

CHILDREN.

VI. (29) Lucy Ann Rosamond, b. Jan. 14, 1833.
(30) Sarah Elisabeth, b. Apr. 22, 1836.
(31) Charles Franklin, b. Jan. 12, 1847.

FIELD.

V. (24) Rhoda W. Lord married April 7, 1843, Simeon C. Field of Northfield, Vt. After living for a time in Boston, Mass., they came to Hanover and now live on the farm which her father and grandfather occupied.

CHILDREN.

VI. (32) Leona Aldana, b. Oct. 1, 1846 ; d. not known.
(33) Bruce Fluellen, b. Oct. 18, 1848.

VI. (33) Bruce F. Field married Josephine M.
Wilmot of Thetford, Vt., November 28, 1877.

CHILDREN.

VII. Charlotte Belle, b. Sept. 30, 1880.
Leonora Alberta, b. Dec. 12, 1887.

SOUTHWICK.

V. (27) Mary Lavina Lord married Lawson
Southwick of Calais, Vt., June, 1847.

CHILD.

VI. (34) Lora Ardena, b. May 1850; d. aged 3 or 4
years.

WALLACE.

V. (27) Mary L. Southwick married (second
time) John Wallace of Leeds, Scotland, March 1862.
Their home has been in South Boston, Mass.

CHILD.

VI. (35) Everean Bruce Lord, b. Sept. 9, 1863.

LORD.

IV. (18) Jonathan Lord married Ruth Hill of
Hanover, N. H., in the winter probably of 1822. She
died in 1850.

CHILDREN.

V. (36) Frances, b. June 1824 ; d. Mar. 22, 1857.
(37) Augusta Marion, b. Aug. 27, 1828.
(38) Wm. Henry Aldis, b. Westville, N. Y., July 26,
1840.

Jonathan Lord lived just south of his father in Hanover, N. H., till about 1832, when he removed to Westville, N. Y., where he lived till his death.

FREEMAN.

V. (36) Frances Lord married December 30, 1847, William H. Freeman of Westville Center, N. Y.

CHILDREN.

VI. Clara, b. Feb. 13, 1851.
Charles, b. Sept. 25, 1854 ; d. Jan. 24, 1858.
Frank, b. March 7, 1857.

RHINEHART.

VI. Clara Freeman married May 20, 1873, John Edward Rhinehart of Westville, N. Y.

CHILDREN.

VII. Arthur, b. Jan. 1, 1875, in Ellenboro, N. Y.
Cora, b. June 9, 1876, in Ellenboro, N. Y.

FREEMAN.

VI. Frank Freeman married April 13, 1881, Emma Josephine Longly.

CHILDREN.

VII. Mabel Augusta, b. Nov. 9, 1886.

This Mr. Freeman is a carpenter and lives at Chicopee Falls, Mass.

HASTINGS.

V. (37) Augusta Marion Lord married Charles Hastings of Malone, N. Y.

CHILDREN.

VI. Arthur G., b. Mar. 21, 1854 ; d. Feb. 4, 1867.
Charles Herbert, b. Jan. 13, 1856.
Frances Marion, b. Feb. 3, 1860 ; d. Dec. 1, 1861.
Clarence Aldis, b. Feb. 22, 1862.
Clara Augusta, b. Sept. 22, 1867.
Nellie Gertrude, b. Oct. 18, 1870 ; d. Aug. 9, 1875.

VI. Charles H. Hastings married January 20, 1877, Carrie Maria Miller.

CHILDREN.

VII. Frank Herbert, b. May 3, 1878.
Gracie Gertrude, b. Mar. 28, 1886, in Utica, N. Y.

Mr. Hastings is a carpenter and builder in partnership with his father at Malone, N. Y.

VI. Clarence A. Hastings married October 7, 1890, Eva M. Clark of Westville, N. Y.

CHILD.

VII. Robert Clark, born, Aug. 4, 1891.

Mr. C. A. Hastings is a practising physician and resides at East Constable, N. Y.

REYNOLDS.

VI. Clara Augusta Hastings married October 1, 1888, Henry H. Reynolds, M. D.

CHILD.

VII. Ruth Marion, b. June 6, 1889.

Mr. Reynolds is a physician in practice at Ellenburgh Depot, N. Y.

LORD.

V. (38) William Henry A. Lord married March 7, 1864, Mary J. Goodspeed of Westville, N. Y. Their home is at Malone, N. Y.

CHILDREN.

VI. Charles G., b. Aug. 20, 1865. This Mr. Lord is a carpenter living in Malone, N. Y.
Katie A., b. Nov. 25, 1867, in Burke, N. Y.
Estella H., b. Dec. 12, 1869.
Elmer E., b. April 21, 1871. This Mr. Lord is a teamster and resides at Malone, N. Y.

DUBY.

VI. Katie A. Lord married August 27, 1890, Walter Duby, a painter. They reside at Watertown, N. Y.

LOMBARD.

VI. Estella H. Lord married February 27, 1889, Darwin Lombard, a farmer, of Beckmantown, N. Y.

CHILD.

VII. Mary H., b. Nov. 27, 1890.

PENNOCK.

III. (6) Experience Lord married, date unknown, a Mr. Pennock. They removed to Craftsbury, Vt., where they lived till the death of both. They had ten children, all daughters. Six of these grew up to womanhood.

IV. (39) Ruth, the eldest, b. date unknown.
(40) Experience, next, "   "
(41) Eunice, next,   "   "
(42) Seraphina, next, "   "
(43) Diadema, next,   "   "
(44) Lavina was youngest, b. date unknown.

GODFREY.

IV. (39) Ruth Pennock married Henry Godfrey, date unknown. Their home is in Chelsea, Vt. No further knowledge.

BROWN.

IV. (40) Experience Pennock married Timothy Brown of Greensboro, Vt. They had ten children. About only one of these is anything known.

V. (45) Chester Brown lived at one time in Hardwick, Vt., as a Methodist minister there.

HYDE.

IV. (41) Eunice Pennock married, date unknown, a Mr. Hyde. They settled in Chelsea, Vt.

WEST.

IV. (42) Seraphina Pennock married, date unknown, a Mr. West. They settled in Vershire, Vt.

HOYT.

IV. (43) Diadema Pennock married, date unknown, Wyman Hoyt of Craftsbury, Vt. They had ten children. Eight of these grew up, three sons and five daughters. In their old age her father and mother came to live with Mr. Hoyt. Mr. Pennock lived to be nearly one hundred years old.

MASON.

IV. (44) Lavina Pennock married, date unknown, Moses Mason of Craftsbury, Vt. They have one son and three daughters. Of Mr. Pennock's other children nothing is known.

LORD.

III. (7) Jonathan Lord married October 14, 1772, Mary Smith. She was born in Hockanum (village), East Hartford, Conn., February 18, 1753; died at Norwich, Vt., June 6, 1831. Her father, Edward Smith, bought land in Windsor Goshen, now Ellington, Conn., in 1752, and moved onto it in 1753, where he lived till 1769, when he came up to Hanover, N. H. His grandfather, Timothy Smith of Hartford, Conn., with a large number of grandchildren, came up to Hanover a few years earlier. According to the family tradition this

Deacon Edward Smith was " bound for a man," and as a result lost his property at East Hartford, Conn., where he had mills, etc., and so left East Hartford for Ellington; and when he came to Hanover he removed his family and household goods in a one-horse wagon. Often at his daughter's, in Norwich, Vt., at family gatherings, he used to say: " What do you think sustained Molly and us under the privations of those times? The hope of better days."

Jonathan Lord made his first home in Strafford, Vt., in 1772; then in the spring before the " Declaration of Independence," he bought of Peter Olcott of Norwich,. Vt., for forty pounds, a fifty acre lot lying on the west side of Pompanoosuc river, and bounded on the north by the south line (as the line then ran) of Thetford, Vt., and on the south by the land of John Rogers, his relative, as was said, Mr. George Burnham having the other fifty acres (of the original one hundred) which lay on the east side of the river. Here he built a log house on the bank of the stream, and so near to it that, as the writer heard his father many a time say, when it was high water they could stand in the door and dip it up. This house stood on land now washed away—in fact, where the middle of the current now flows—and almost exactly opposite the front of the meeting-house in Union Village. While living in this house, and his father in the log house on the meadow further to the south, the family tradition says meat was sometimes scarce, and at one of these times " a bear was killed on the Pompanoosuc river, weighing five hundred pounds." Of course

it was shared among these families, and the one who
gave the report of it said, "You may be sure it went
well."

In 1786 Jonathan Lord built a frame house on the
west side of the road, as it then ran north and south
through the town and on a rise of land sloping beau-
tifully down to the road, but when the turnpike was
put through the town, it left this house on the east side
of it. This house stood a short distance north of the
house formerly owned by E. G. Lord. Here he and
his wife lived till their death.

After Mr. Lord got into his new house he began to
raise an abundance of excellent wheat, and so had wheat
to sell. One day a buyer came to look at some grain.
Mr. Lord took him up into the chamber where the
wheat was stored in tierces. While the man was ex-
amining the grain Mr. Lord said : " Pretty good wheat,
pretty good wheat." As the man made no response, Mr.
Lord said with great emphasis, " Pretty good wheat, I
say ! "

CHILDREN.

IV. (45) Porter, b. in Strafford, Vt., Aug. 10, 1775 ; d.
in Orange, Vt., Feb. 23, 1856.

(46) Russell, b. in Norwich, Vt., June 4, 1777 ; d. in
Thetford, Vt., Jan. 17, 1833.

(47) John, b. (in that log house) Aug. 1, 1782 ; d.
June 19, 1882, aged 100 years, lacking 42
days.

(48) Mary (Polly), b. Feb. 1, 1785 ; d. May 31, 1827.

(49) Lydia, b. June 1, 1787 ; d. March 18, 1851.

(50) Rachel, b. about 1790 ; d. in childhood.

IV. (45) Porter Lord married Sophia Locke at Norwich, Vt., January 14, 1795. She was the daughter of James Locke; was born in Townsend, Mass., December 11, 1773; died in Orange, Vt., December 6, 1868. She had come to Norwich, Vt., with some of her brothers, who as millwrights were engaged in building the first grist-mill erected in Union Village; one of these brothers, by the fall of a millstone, received an injury which resulted in his death.

Porter Lord removed from Norwich to Orange, Vt., in April, 1797, when his oldest daughter was six weeks old, going through Corinth; as they all went those early years, he himself having gone the previous autumn and built a log house. His father, who had assisted him in getting and buying the land, went with him to assist in putting up the house. In this house he lived seventeen and a half years. It stood down near the road in front of the new one, and some of the old cellar remains there still. Originally, one hundred acres of land lying in another part of the town had been bargained for, but, as they failed to get a good title to it, it was exchanged for the ninety-five acres on which he settled. After they came the first frame house in town was erected, it being raised by twelve or thirteen men, five or six of whom only lived in town, the others coming from Washington or Barre, the house being erected in the southwestern part of the town. When Mr. Lord and his wife came to Orange it was an almost unbroken wilderness, and they suffered many privations incident to first settlers in the newer parts of the country. On the same farm on to which they first removed they lived till a good old age, being respected and beloved as citizens and pillars, or active supporters, of the Methodist Episcopal Church in town, the wife outliving her husband nearly twelve years, amid many infirmities of body and the loss of sight. Their youngest son had his home also on this same farm with them.

CHILDREN.

V. (51) Porter, b. Norwich, Vt., Apr. 14, 1796; d. June 1, 1796.
   (52) Sophia, b. Norwich, Vt., Mar. 25, 1797; d. Apr. 21, 1888.
   (53) Clarissa, b. Jan. 1, 1800; d. Sept. 20, 1802.
   (54) Maria, b. May 2, 1802; d. Jan. 9, 1843.
   (55) Clarissa, b. Nov. 4, 1803; d. Mar. 21, 1813.
   (56) Mary, b. Jan. 15, 1806; d. Jan. 6, 1888.
   (57) Porter Locke, b. Jan. 9, 1809; d. Mar. 26, 1893.
   (58) John Proctor, b. May 29, 1813; d. May 21, 1892.
   (59) Eleazer Wells, b. May 10, 1815; d. Aug. 3, 1877.
   (60) Angeline Farnsworth, b. Sept. 29, 1817; d. about Apr. 30, 1897.

TILLOTSON.

V. (52) Sophia Lord married December 9, 1821, Lester Tillotson of Orange, Vt.

CHILDREN.

VI. (61) Lester M., b. Topsham, Vt., Dec. 23, 1823; d. Sept. 17, 1824.
   (62) Chester B., b. Topsham, Vt., Aug. 6, 1824.
   (63) Sophia Locke, b. Topsham, Vt., July 26, 1826; d. Sept. 30, 1843.

(64) Orlando M., b. Orange, Vt., Aug. 28, 1828; d.
Oct. 7, 1864.
(65) Oramel M., b. Orange, Vt., Aug. 26, 1831; d.
May 5, 1864.
(66) Albinus Lester, b. Orange, Vt., Aug. 1, 1832.
(67) Eveline, b. Orange, Vt., June 30, 1835; d. 1880.
(68) Mary E., b. Orange, Vt., Nov. 20, 1838.
(69) Malvina, b. Elmore, Vt., Oct. 6, 1844; d. Apr.
12, 1902.

VI. (62) Chester B. Tillotson married February
25, 1847, at Manchester, N. H., Elvira Herrington.
He lives at East Montpelier, Vt. She died July, 1897.

CHILDREN.

VII. (70) Son, b. Elmore, Vt., Dec. 17, 1849; d. same day.
(71) Son, b. Elmore, Vt., 1851; d. same day.
(72) Olin L., b. Elmore, Vt., July 3, 1854.
(73) Chester F., b. Wolcott, Vt., Apr. 2, 1859.
(74) Son, b. Wolcott, Vt., July 19, 1863; d. July
26, 1863.
(75) Melora, b. Wolcott, Vt., Feb. 21, 1865.

VI. (64) Orlando M. Tillotson married February
26, 1850, at Elmore, Vt., Marilla Olmstead.

CHILDREN.

VII. (76) Son, b. Wolcott, Vt., May 2, 1852; d. June 2,
1852.
(77) Cora L., b. Wolcott, Vt., Sept. 8, 1853.
(78) Hattie A., b. Wolcott, Vt., June 18, 1855.
(79) Emma S., b. Wolcott, Vt., July 1, 1858.
(80) Lester L., b. Wolcott, Vt., Aug. 11, 1860.

Their father was a member of Company D, Eleventh Regiment of Vermont Volunteers and died at Lincoln Hospital, Germantown, Pa.

VI. (65) Oramel M. Tillotson married April 13, 1856, at Craftsbury, Vt., Martha Ann Sprague.

CHILDREN.

VII. (81) George L., b. Wolcott, Vt., Feb. 27, 1857.
   (82) William S., b. Wolcott, Vt., June 6, 1859.
   (83) Martha J., b. Wolcott, Vt., Aug. 10, 1862.

Their father was a member of Company E, Third Regiment Vermont Volunteers, and died in the Battle of the Wilderness, May 5, 1864.

VI. (66) Albinus Lester Tillotson married May 20, 1855, at Wolcott, Vt., Mary W. Davis.

CHILDREN.

VII. (84) Isabel May, b. Wolcott, Vt., Sept. 28, 1857.
   (85) Nellie S., b. Wolcott, Vt., Nov. 28, 1858.
   (86) Clara Ann, b. Wolcott, Vt., April 19, 1860.
   (87) George A., b. Wolcott, Vt., Feb. 5, 1861.
   (88) Sarah L., b. Wolcott, Vt., Sept. 22, 1863.
   (89) Oramel O., b. Wolcott, Vt., May 4, 1869.
   (90) William L., b. Wolcott, Vt., Sept. 28, 1871.

SAWYER.

VI. (67) Eveline A. Tillotson married Nov. 25, 1856, at Manchester, N. H., Zara Sawyer.

CHILDREN.

VII. (91) Fred A., b. Manchester, N. H., Nov. 25, 1857.
   (92) Elmer E., b. Manchester, N. H., Nov. 25, 1861.

LANGLEY.

VI. (68) Mary E. Tillotson married February 13, 1862, at Wolcott, Vt., John Langley of Manchester, N. H.

CHILD.

VII. (93) Mary Della, b. Wolcott, Vt., April 1, 1868.

BROWN.

VI. (69) Malvina M. Tillotson married December 15, 1860, Albert Brown of Wolcott, Vt.

CHILD.

VII. (94) Angeline, b. Wolcott, Vt., June 22, 1866.

BEARD.

V. (56) Mary Lord married April 4, 1825, at Orange, Vt., Benjamin Beard.

CHILDREN.

VI. (94a) Clarissa, b. Orange, Vt., Dec. 15, 1825.
  (95) William F., b. Orange, Vt., June 3, 1828.
  (96) Urania, b. Orange, Vt., Jan. 22, 1831 ; d. Sublette, Ill., Dec. 30, 1858.
  (97) Joseph W., b. Orange, Vt., July 6, 1835 ; d. Sublette, Ill., Jan. 9, 1859.
  (98) Calvin L., b. Orange, Vt., Nov. 28, 1839 ; d. Feb. 14, 1862, at Bird's Point, Mo., a member of Seventh Illinois Cavalry.
  (99) Elwin A., b. Albany, Vt., Sept. 28, 1852.

This Mr. Benjamin Beard, born in Orange, Vt., was for many years a minister of the Methodist Episcopal Church in Vermont before his removal to Sublette, Lee county, Ill., where he resided for a long time.

VI. (95) William F. Beard married in Sublette, Ill., March 23, 1854, Mary L. Bassett.

CHILDREN.

VII. (100) Alice E., b. Jan. 3, 1855.
(101) Oscar F., b. April 23, 1858.
(102) Abbie W., b. Dec. 16, 1859.
(103) Edgar W., b. Aug. 10, 1861.
(104) Charles B., b. Jan. 19, 1864.
(105) Milton E., b. Mar. 2, 1872; d. Sept. 29, 1872.

LORD.

V. (57) Porter L. Lord married May 1, 1835, at Orange, Vt., Martha N. Pike.

CHILDREN (BY ADOPTION).

VI. (106) Delia P., b. May 8, 1842.
(107) Hattie M., b. May 13, 1855.

Mr. Lord was a cabinet-maker by trade and was also the only undertaker in Orange for more than fifty years. He was a man noted for his sterling character and close adherence to business, always winning friends wherever his duties called him.

CURTIS.

VI. (106) Delia P. Lord married December 25, 1865, at Orange, Vt., Mason B. Curtis.

CHILDREN.

VII. (108) Morna Ellen, b. July 10, 1866; d. Sept. 14, 1879.
(109) Agnes Martha, b. June 12, 1870.
(110) Mary Bessie, b. April 11, 1872.
(111) Fred Mason, b. Nov. 25, 1880.

LORD.

V. (58) John P. Lord married October 20, 1839, Emily White of Orange.

VI. (112) Raymond Porter, b. Mar. 5, 1843.
(113) Constance A., b. July 29, 1844 ; d. Dec. 10, 1845.
(114) Daughter, b. Sept. 5, 1845 ; d. same day.
(115) Florence S., b. May 5, 1847 ; d. Sept. 1, 1857.
(116) Coraline, b. April 8, 1849.
(117) Lenora C., b. Jan. 28, 1852.
(118) John L., b. Mar. 27, 1854.
(119) Emma C., b. Oct. 3, 1859 ; d. Mar. 27, 1860.

Emily White Lord died July 25, 1860.

Married (second time) Elizabeth (Colburn) Bailey of Plainfield, Vt.

VI. (120) Edith M., b. June 18, 1863.
(121) Charles C., b. Aug. 29, 1864.
(122) Justin Morrill, b. Mar. 24, 1866.

Mr. John P. Lord was a blacksmith by trade, and for many years the only one in the town of Orange. He was a man of pleasing nature, of a quiet jovial humor, and withal a man of much influence in the town.

VI. (112) Raymond Porter Lord married February 24, 1867, Keziah Guild of Coventry, Vt.

CHILDREN.

VII. (123) Nettie E., b. Jan. 30, 1868.
(124) James W., b. May 11, 1871.
Luther R., b. Aug. 21, 1874.
Lizzie E., b. Jan. 27, 1878; d. April 21, 1882.
Dan Guild, b. Sept. 5, 1883.

CAVE.

VII. (123) Nettie E. Lord married May 16, 1889,
Mr. Walter J. Cave.

CHILD.

VIII. Osmond E., b. March 23, 1896.

LORD.

VII. (124) James W. Lord married August 21,
1895, Eva G. Nelson.

CHILD.

VIII. Fern E., b. Jan. 15, 1900.

Eva G. Nelson died February 16, 1900.

BATCHELDER.

VI. (116) Coraline Lord married April 11, 1867,
Zenas Batchelder of Montpelier, Vt.

CHILDREN.

VII. (125) Wendal H., b. April 28, 1868; d. May 7, 1868.
(126) Ernest LeRoy, b. Feb. 28, 1869 (or 1872).

Mr. Batchelder died October 6, 1873.

TOWER.

VI. (116) Coraline Batchelder married (second time), September 9, 1886, Benjamin Tower of Coventry, Vt.

Mr. Towers' business is that of a merchant. He died August, 1897.

GUILD.

VI. (117) Lenora Constance Lord married June 24, 1875, Luther Guild of Coventry, Vt.

CHILDREN.

VII. Raymond Lord, b. Feb. 24, 1879.
Marion Edith, b. Oct. 23, 1880.
Warren Locke, b. Dec. 3, 1882.

LORD.

VI. (118) John Locke Lord married October 6, 1876, Cemira E. Guild of Coventry, Vt.

CHILDREN.

VII. Theron Arthur, b. May 16, 1879.
Leon Bertie, b. April 18, 1881.
Fred Ernest, b. Oct. 27, 1883.
Jane Sophronia, b. Oct. 10, 1885.
Amos Jasper, b. Aug. 17, 1890.
Minnie E., b. Sept. 4, 1893.

WINSLOW.

VI. (120) Edith M. Lord married June 18, 1889, D. L. Winslow of North Brookfield, Mass.

CHILD.

Jennie Lord, b. May 23, 1895.

LORD.

VI. (121) Charles Colburn Lord married June 19, 1889, Ettie M. Wilds.

CHILDREN.

VII. Ralph C., b. May 19, 1890.

Wendell E., b. Aug 19, 1894; lives at West Groton, Vt., and is editor of the Groton Times.

VI. (122) Justin M. Lord married December 24, 1890, Hattie B. Eastman.

CHILDREN.

VII. Elizabeth A., b. Oct. 4, 1892.
Clarence, b. Sept. 5, 1897.

V. (59) Eleazer W. Lord married January 8, 1845, at Orange, Sophronia White (sister of Emily White, mentioned above), who died October 24, 1848.

CHILD.

VI. (127) Bernard E., b. Oct. 8, 1848; d. Sept. 2, 1877.

He married (second time) March 27, 1849, Orinda White (sister of the first wife).

CHILDREN.

VI. (128) Sophronia M., b. Feb. 16, 1850.
(129) Lella M., b. Jan. 25, 1852.
(130) Reuben P., b. March 12, 1855.
(131) Emma W., b. May 2, 1861.
(132) Mary E., b. Oct. 6, 1864; d. Aug. 10, 1877.
(133) Marion J., b. Sept. 14, 1866.

VI. (127) Bernard E. Lord married May 21, 1872, Abbie Wood of Mendon, Mass. After his death she married a Mr. Peabody of Orange, Vt.

COFFIN.

VI. (128) Sophronia M. Lord married January 1, 1867, Ferdinand D. S. Coffin of Orange, Vt.

CHILDREN.

VII. (134) Glen M., b. Jan. 2, 1870.
(135) Aldee B., b. March 26, 1872.

TAYLOR.

VI. (129) Lella M. Lord married November 29, 1883, Noah C. Taylor of Washington, Vt.

CHILDREN.

VII. Nora E., b. Oct. 21, 1884.
Florence O., b. June 24, 1886.
Clinton, b. March, 1887 ; d. Sept. 13, 1887.
Harvey A., b. July 14, 1888.
Jasper E., b. Aug. 11, 1890.

LORD.

VI. (130) Reuben P. Lord married February 14, 1902, Mabel Barrup.

SANDERS.

VI. (131) Emma W. Lord married September 25, 1880, Charles Sanders of Washington, Vt.

CHILDREN.

VII. Louis, b. Jan. 13, 1884.
Mamie, b. March 16, 1889.
Their home has been Nashua, N. H.

LORD.

IV. (46) Russell Lord married December 6, 1798, Sarah Marshall of Thetford, Vt. She was born September 4, 1777; died October 10, 1847.

CHILDREN.

V. (134a) Reuben Marshall, b. Sept. 7, 1779 ; d. May 25, 1857.
(135a) Russell, b. May 17, 1801 ; d. Aug. 13, 1879.
(136) Sarah, b. Sept. 4, 1803 ; d. Dec. 17, 1805.
(137) Jasper, b. Oct. 4, 1805 ; d. Jan. 26, 1875.
(138) Eliza, b. Jan. 24, 1810 ; d. July 1, 1815.
(139) A daughter, b. Aug. 30, 1819 ; d. Sept. 7, 1819.

Mr. Russell Lord made for himself a home on a farm on the west branch of the Ompompanoosuc river in West Thetford, Vt., where he lived and died, and where his second son lived and died.

V. (134a) Reuben M. Lord married December 23, 1823, Lucinda, daughter of James and Mary Moore of Thetford, Vt. She afterwards married (second time) a Mr. Morse of Jefferson, N. H. ; died in 1881.

CHILDREN.

VI. (140) Sarah E., b. May 26, 1825 ; d. Aug. 26, 1856.
(141) Lucena-L., b. May 26, 1828.
(142) James Harris, b. Nov. 30, 1831 ; d. Dec. 3, 1831.
(143) Frances L., b. July 20, 1834 ; d. about 1885.
(144) Harriet M., b. Dec. 25, 1838 ; d. Dec. 16, 1892.

TEELE.

VI. (140) Sarah E. Lord married October 10, 1852, Rev. Edwin Teele, at Somerville, Mass. They had been appointed as missionaries by the A. B. C. F. M., and in December following they started for the Fairfield station, Indian Territory, Cherokee nation. In September of 1853, she was taken with chills and fever. Then her sister, Lucena L., went out to assist in the family. In October, 1854, her health continuing poor, and Mr. Teele's health failing, they returned to Thetford, Vt. She improved in health during 1855, but in 1856 the disease assumed a more threatening form, and after her infant son died she gradually sank away till her "mortal put on immortality," Aug. 26, 1856.

CHILDREN.

VII. (145) Sarah, b. (1853).
    (146) Edwin, b. July, 1855 ; d. June, 1856.

FROST.

VI. (141) Lucena L. Lord married September 12, 1855, Warren S. Frost of Belmont, Mass.

CHILDREN.

VII. (147) J. Newton, b. Sept. 24, 1856 ; drowned in Florida Dec. 22, 1878.
    (148) Walter Lord, b. Oct. 16, 1859.
           Lucena Moore, b. Sept. 22, 1861.
           Carlton Shattuck, b. Sept. 27, 1864.

VII. (148) Walter L. Frost married October 7, 1891, Etta L. Eastman of Hollis, N. H.

CHILDREN.

VIII. Walter Eastman, b. Nov. 30, 1893.
Katherine Lord, b. July 28, 1896.

WEST.

VI. (143) Frances L. Lord married December 7, 1854, at Thetford, Vt., Presbury West, 3d.

CHILDREN.

VII. (151) Mary Burton, b. Lisbon, Wis., Jan. 7, 1866; d. same day.
(152) William Lord, b. Dec. 15, 1858.
(153) Henry Merritt, b. about 1860; d. 1866.
(154) Fannie, b. Nov. 3, 1865.

MORSE.

VI. (144) Harriet M. Lord married November 4, 1857, at Lancaster, N. H., John M. Morse.

CHILDREN.

VII. (155) Merritt Presby, b. Lancaster, N. H., Sept. 20, 1862.
(156) Ernest L., b. Sept. 13, 1870.

Mr. Reuben M. Lord always had his home in Thetford, Vt., though in three different places. Himself, wife and all his daughters were members of the Old First (Cong.) Church in town.

LORD.

V. (135a) Russell Lord, 2d, married January 18, 1827, Caroline Moore, sister of his older brother's wife.

CHILD.

VI. (157) Mary Laurette, b. Aug. 15, 1830.

V. (137) Jasper Lord married March 4, 1830, Alpa B. West of Thetford Center. They made their home in West Thetford. He was a farmer and also a mason by trade.

BUZZELL.

VI. (157) Mary Laurette Lord married October 11, 1860, James Webster Buzzell, of some town in New Hampshire.

LORD.

IV. (47) John Lord married December 16, 1813, Lucy Bliss. She was the daughter of David and Lucy (Stebbins) Bliss, both of Springfield, Mass. She was born in Hartford, Conn., January 17, 1789; died in Norwich, Vt., July 28, 1872.

CHILDREN.

V. (158) David Bliss, b. Nov. 14, 1814; d. Dec. 16, 1869.
(159) Jonathan Smith, b. Aug. 31, 1816; d. June 14, 1882.
(160) Lucius Stebbins, b. Sept. 7, 1818; d. Jan. 31, 1900.

4

(161) John Mills, b. Wednesday, October 4, 1820; d. ——.

(162) Harriet Ann, b. Apr. 1, 182❓ d. ——

(163) Horatio Flagg, b. Dec. 26, 1826 ; d. Apr. 11, 1832.

(164) Judah Albinus, b. Sept. 9, 1829 ; d. Mar. 11, 1832.

(165) Lucy Isabel, b. Apr. 21, 1832.

Mr. John Lord lived with his father till after his marriage. The first land he bought after becoming of age was the farm of his great uncle (as was supposed), John Rodgers, and which lay between the farm of James Waterman on the south and his father's on the north. He fitted up the house on this place for his own residence and here all his children were born. He lived and died on the farm on which he had been born. When he had lived ninety and nine years and was still active and vigorous, the good people of the vicinity were quite anxious he should complete his full one hundred years that they might be able to celebrate his hundredth anniversary, but in this they were disappointed, for, without any disease, he passed away a month and eleven days before he reached the full century. He was like a clock which, having been wound up to run a century, run on till it was completely run down, and then stopped. So he died in a good old age, having been a member of the Congregational Church more than sixty years.

V. (158) David B. Lord married January 6, 1863, Mary Elisabeth Howard of Norwich, Vt. She died November 28, 1897, at Norwich, Vt.

51 .

CHILDREN.

VI. (166) Lucy Elizabeth, b. Jan. 14, 1864.
(167) Sarah Ellen, b. Mar. 25, 1867.

JENKS.

VI. (166) Lucy E. Lord married September 4, 1887, John E. Jenks of Fairlee, Vt.

CHILDREN.

VII. (168) Mary Amanda, b. Feb. 12, 1888.
(169) Helen Elizabeth, b. Sept. 15, 1889.
David Elmer, b. Apr. 2, 1892 ; d. July 19, 1893.
Lawrence, b. June 23, 1894 ; d. Oct. 5, 1894.
Leon Ralph, b. Aug. 17, 1895.
Katherine, b. June 11, 1899 ; d. June 18, 1899.
Marion Walker and Margaret Bliss, b. Sept. 19, 1901.
Margaret Bliss, d. Oct. 14, 1901.
Marion Walker, d. Sept. 22, 1902.

WOODS.

VI. (167) Ellen Sarah Lord married September 4, 1886, Clarence S. Woods of Concord, N. H.

LORD.

V. (159) Jonathan Smith Lord married May 9, 1839, Laura Lord, daughter of Deacon Asa Lord of Norwich, Vt.

CHILDREN.

VI. (170) Mary Lundie, b. June 29, 1850 ; d. Apr. 4, 1866.
(171) Ann Thane, b. Aug. 24, 1852 ; d. Sept. 6, 1852.
(172) Grace Elizabeth, b. Jan. 24, 1856.
(173) Edwin Goodell, b. Aug. 29, 1859.
(174) Henry Holdane, b. Mar. 9, 1861 ; d. Apr. 21, 1865.

CHILD.

VI. (172) Grace E. Lord married May 24, 1879, Bela Child of Thetford, Vt. He died July 3, 1879.

LORD.

VI. (172) Grace E. Child married (second time) March 13, 1884, William Wilberforce Lord of Somonauk, La Salle county, Ill.

CHILDREN.

VII. (175) Jessie Margarette, b. May 6, 1886
Ruth Helen, b. Nov. 1892.

Mr. William W. Lord was killed by the kick of a horse, on the head.

FOWLER.

Mrs. Grace E. Lord was married (third time) to John C. Fowler of East Richmond, Va., November 4, 1897. Mr. Fowler is a large farmer near Richmond, Va.

VI. (173) Edwin G. Lord married March 4, 1882, Jennie Elizabeth Cloud of Norwich, Vt.

CHILDREN.

VII. (176) Grace Elizabeth, b. Feb. 21, 1883.
(177) Bessie Glee, b. Oct. 19, 1887.

V. (160) Lucius S. Lord married May 1, 1851, Alpa Rosette Little of Norwich, Vt.

CHILDREN.

VI. (178) Abbie Sanborn, b. Aug. 1, 1853; d. Feb. 18, 1859.
(179) Alpa Rosette, b. Oct. 23, 1855; d. Nov. 5, 1890.
(180) John Franklin, b. Jan. 29, 1860.
Eliza Nelson, b. Mar. 9, 1869.

RUGGLES.

VI. (179) Alpa R. Lord married November 1889, Frederick A. Ruggles of Norwich, Vt.

LORD.

VI. (180) John F. Lord married September 18, 1888, Ida M. Richards of Sioux City, Iowa.

CHILDREN.

VII. (181) Russell Carlton, b. July 13, 1889.
Alicia Rosette, b. Oct. 25, 1892.
Helen Norene, b. Jan. 23, 1894.

V. (161) John Mills Lord married September 12, 1861, Harriet Billings, daughter of Phineas C. Butterfield, Esq., of Francestown, N. H.

Mr. John M. Lord pursued his preparatory studies at Thetford Academy, Thetford, Vt., and entered Dartmouth College in 1840, graduating in course in 1844. After teaching one year in Kentucky he entered Lane Theological Seminary, Cincinnati, Ohio, in the autumn of 1845, and graduated in 1848. In 1849 he preached for the Second Congregational Church and Society, Brookfield, Vt. In the spring of 1851 he went down onto the seashore for his health and preached three years for the Church and Society of North Truro, Mass., where by a council he was ordained to the work of the ministry, December 21, 1851. Soon afterwards he gathered the Congregational Church that now is in Wilmington, Vt., leaving them in 1858 with seventy-two members.

After this he preached a longer or shorter time for churches in several other towns in different states, never having been installed, although he had received ten or more calls to be the pastor or to be installed over as many different churches, but having declined them nearly all, chiefly on account of continued ill health. In 1863 he received a severe injury to his back by being thrown from a carriage, and this was the cause of a great amount of suffering and weakness for many years. Because of this he sought a home in several different places, in seeking a change of climate, and because of it also he engaged in teaching at three different times and places, while suffering from great debility many long years.

DUTTON.

V. (162) Harriet Ann Lord married June 14, 1848, John Dutton of Norwich, Vt. He was the son of Daniel B. and Lorana (Smith) Dutton. He was born at Stowe, Vt., August 23, 1818; died in Norwich, Vt., January 16, 1888.

CHILDREN.

VI. (182) Louisa Augusta, b. Oct. 16, 1851; d. Jan. 21, 1863.

(183) George Albinus, b. Sept. 15, 1854; d. June 6, 1885.

(184) Charles Sumner, b. Dec. 9, 1857.

(185) Henry Allen, b. Aug. 4, 1860; d. Mar. 15, 1868.

(186) Hattie Elizabeth, b. Feb. 22, 1863.

(187) Mary Lorana, b. Jan. 4, 1868; d. March 3, 1868.

VI. (183) George A. Dutton pursued his college preparatory studies first at the Academy in his native town, and then at the Academy at St. Johnsbury, Vt.; entered Dartmouth college in 1876, and graduated in course in 1880; three years later he graduated from the Theological Seminary, Hartford, Conn.; in the autumn following, September 6, he was ordained to the work of the ministry at Norwich, Vt.; preached about six months for the Congregational Church of Weston, Vt., and then left for missionary work in the employ of A. B. C. F. Missions in Mexico, where he arrived April 11, 1884. In about a year he had so learned the Spanish language as to use it with facility, when he was stricken down with the smallpox, and after a severe illness he died at Chihuahua, Mexico, June 6, 1885.

VI. (184) Charles S. Dutton fitted for college at the Academy in Norwich, Vt., and graduated from the Chandler Department of Dartmouth College in 1880. He married Ella Frances Lyman of Norwich, November 22, 1884.

CHILDREN.

VII. (188) Mabel Frances, b. Oct. 4, 1885.
      (189) Alice Lyman, b. July 20, 1887.
             George Augustus, b. Aug. 13, 1893.
             Mary, b. May 5, 1898.

METCALF.

VI. (186) Hattie E. Dutton married Otis Metcalf, January 23, 1889.

56

CHILDREN.

VII. (190) Frederic Ernest, b. Jan. 4, 1890.
Florence Dutton, b. Jan. 11, 1892 ; d. Sept. 10,
1892.
Paul, b. July 28, 1893.

CHANDLER.

V. (165) Lucy Isabel Lord married at Norwich,
Vt., September 4, '1860, Rev. Augustus Chandler of
Woodstock, Conn. He graduated at Williams College
in 1855, and at Andover Theological Seminary 1859.
He preached first for a year at Saxton's River, Vt. ;
then for the Congregational Church of Lempster, N. H. ;
afterwards he was settled over the Congregational
Church of Strafford, Vt., and then over that of Dummerston, Vt. At a later date he preached in other
places, as his health would permit, till he became
editor and proprietor of an agricultural journal, the
Record and Farmer, at Brattleboro, Vt. This he continued till he died there of pneumonia, March 26, 1880.

CHILDREN.

VI. (191) Mary Elizabeth, b. at Lempster, N. H., Oct.
30, 1861.
(192) Benjamin F., b. at Dummerston, Vt., Feb. 25,
1870.
(193) John Lord, b. Brattleboro, Vt., Feb. 13, 1876.

TOPLIFF.

VI. (191) Mary E. Chandler married —— Topliff of South Coventry, Conn.

CHILD.

VII. (194) A son.

PROCTOR.

IV. (49) Lydia Lord married May 5, 1808, at Norwich, Vt., John Proctor. He was born November 2, 1781; died July 3, 1812.

CHILDREN.

V. (195) Louisa Lord, b. about 1810; d. about 1825.
(196) Ann Turner, b. Jan. 7, 1812; d. March 31, 1887.

BRIGHAM.

V. (196) Ann T. Proctor married September 26, 1832, William Brigham of Norwich, Vt. He died April 18, 1889.

CHILDREN.

VI. (197) Charlotte E., b. Aug. 10, 1833; d. June 30, 1859.
(198) Ellen Amanda, b. Oct. 6, 1835; d. Apr. 2, 1857.
(199) John Proctor, b. Jan. 3, 1838; d. Jan. 11, 1840.
(200) Frances A., b. Mar. 12, 1840; d. Oct. 16, 1856.
(201) Louisa A., b. Feb. 18, 1842.
(202) William Andrew, b. Jan. 30, 1847.
(203) Albert C., b. Sept. 28, 1849.

VI. (202) William Andrew Brigham married February 4, 1868, Abbie S. Johnson of Norwich, Vt.

CHILDREN.

VII. (204) Annie Adaline, b. Feb. 3, 1869.
(205) Grace Louisa, b. Mar. 5, 1872.
(206) William Edwin, b. June 12, 1875.
(207) Paul Andrew, b. Feb. 9, 1883.

VI. (203) Albert C. Brigham married Alice
Maxum of Worcester, Vt., September 23, 1872.

CHILD.

VII. (208) Mary Alice, b. Mar. 13, 1875.

The mother of Mary Alice died January 4, 1889.

CHAMBERLAIN.

III. (8) Ruth Lord married about 1773 Mr. Reuben Chamberlain, probably of Lebanon, N. H. At the
present time no further knowledge of him remains or
of the time of his death.

IV. (209) They had one son, Reuben. In 1775
his mother married again. This son when old enough
went south and entered the United States Army. A very
interesting letter from him to a relative in the north,
dated "Fort Adams, Mississippi Territory, June 15,
1808," (This fort was on the east bank of the Mississippi river,) informs us that at that time he was a lieutenant in the army and expecting soon to be promoted
to the office of captain. He earnestly asks for information of every kind, relating to his father of whom he
was in utter ignorance. He complains that as an
"infant" he was received into the home of his stepfather without a father's love or tenderness or welcome,
that this step-father soon removed him to the home of
the step-father's brother, where, without love or tenderness, he was "suffered to vegetate" up to youth.

Another account says he continued in the army, and after the close of the war of 1812, in its peace establishment, he was stationed at St. Stevens, Alabama, where he married in 1820.

CHILDREN.

V. (210) A son, who died in infancy.
(211) Pendleton, b. in 1822.
(212) Rubana, b. in 1824.
(213) Frances Henrietta, b. in 1826.
(214) Toulmin, b. in 1828.

One of these sons was educated at the Military Academy, West Point, N. Y.

TILDEN.

III. Ruth Chamberlain married the second time Joseph Tilden of Lebanon, N. H. This was also his second marriage. Soon after, he bought a farm one mile south of Hanover Plain (or if not he, then his eldest son did). He was born at Bolton, Conn., in 1746; died in Lebanon, N. H., April, 1824. After his death his widow made her home with her son Timothy, in Norwich, Vt., where she died.

CHILDREN.

IV. (215) Joseph, b. Nov. 18, 1778; d. Hanover, N. H., Mar. 22, 1861.
(216) Ruth, b. Feb. 1, 1780.
(217) Lydia, b. Nov. 15, 1781; d. Aug. 2, 1860.
(218) Elisha, b. Nov. 14, 1783; d. Apr. 13, 1863.
(219) John, b. Nov. 28, 1785.
(220) Phebe, b. Nov. 5, 1788.

(221) Timothy, b. May 26, 1791 ; d. Oct. 26, 1879.
(222) Joel, b. July 22, 1793 ; d. in California about
         1866.
(223) Titus, b. about 1795 ; d. about 1812.

IV. (215) Joseph Tilden married January 5, 1804,
Betsey Woodward.

CHILDREN.

V. (224) Emily, b. July 11, 1805 ; d. ——.
    (225) Lydia, b. Sept. 19, 1806 ; d. ——.
    (226) Edna, b. March 8, 1809 ; d. Aug. 24, 1813.
    (227) Betsey, b. Nov. 22, 1810 ; d. Feb. 11, 1890.
    (228) Joseph, b. Oct. 12, 1812 ; d. Oct. 25, 1812.
    (229) Joseph, b. Feb. 5, 1814 ; d. ——.
    (230) Titus Woodward, b. Nov. 15, 1816 ; d. ——.

V. (227) This daughter Betsey was for nearly
seven years a missionary in Palestine in the employ of
the A. B. C. Foreign Missions.

V. (229) Joseph Tilden married October, 1842,
Mary Virgin ; married (second time) April, 1868, Mrs.
Lydia E. Spencer.

V. (230) Titus W. Tilden graduated from Dartmouth College in the class of 1842 (I think). After
his graduation he went west as a teacher, in northern
Ohio, and his residence (it is believed) is in or near
Sandusky, Ohio. He married Mary Elisabeth Chrism-
bury of northern Ohio.

CHILDREN.

VI. (231) Emma Josephine, b. ——.
     (232) Charles, b. ——.
     (233) Titus Woodward, b. ——.

IV. (216) Ruth Tilden married James Kendrick of Hanover, N. H.

BARTLETT.

IV. (217) Lydia Tilden married Jairus Bartlett of Norwich, Vt. He had his home on a farm on the north side of the Pompanoosuc river, a little back from the meadow, and a short distance up the stream from what is now Patterson's Flat.

V. (234) They had one son, John. After the death of his father and mother he lived unmarried in their old house, some of the time having a family in the house with him, and carrying on the farm in his fashion for about ten years, when suddenly he disappeared, not far from 1870, and never being seen again was supposed by many to have been murdered.

TILDEN.

IV. (218) Elisha Tilden married Sophia Ordway, and afterwards Lucretia Ordway. He had his home on a farm about a mile northwest of Thetford Hill, in Thetford, Vt.

CHILDREN.

V. (235) Finette, b. ——.
   (236) Melissa, b. ——.

It is believed they had a son younger.

IV. (219) John Tilden married Sally Ellis. Children, seven sons; names unknown. He had his home in Lebanon, N. H., till he removed west, where he died.

WATERMAN.

IV. (220) Phebe Tilden married Daniel Waterman
of Norwich, Vt. He had his home on the south side
of the Pompanoosuc river, and a little above the lower
bridge; some years before he died he sold his farm and
removed to the Flat. Children:

V. Four daughters that lived to grow up, one of
whom (eldest perhaps) married A. [Asa?] Cummings
of Thetford, Vt.

VI. They have several children.

TILDEN.

IV. (221) Timothy Tilden married Sophia Frarey
of Lebanon, N. H. She died April 21, 1872. Mr.
Tilden's farm was on the east side of Norwich, Vt.,
about midway north and south, and some distance back
from the Connecticut river. Among other things that
may be said of him is this: He began to attend the
commencement exercises of Dartmouth College when
five years old, and he attended every one afterwards as
long as he lived, making eighty-three times.

CHILDREN.

V. (235a) Reuben Chamberlain, b. May 1, 1817.
(236a) Timothy, b. June 5, 1818; d. Hanover, N. H.,
Sept. 22, 1870.
(237) Fannie Frarey, b. Feb. 12, 1820; d. ——.
(238) Sophia, b. Nov. 4, 1821; d. ——.
(239) Lois Louisa, b. March 6, 1824; d. ——.
(240) Verona, b. July 14, 1825; d. ——.

(241)   Elvira, b. March 28, 1827 ; d. Oct. 4, 1845.
(242)   Ruth, b. March 20, 1829 ; d. ——.
(243)   Theta, b. Jan. 21, 1831 ; d. ——.
(244)   Ransom, b. July 28, 1834 ; d. April 30, 1835.
(245)   Jane L., b. April 2, 1836.
(246)   Mary Sophia, b. April 23, 1848.
(247)   Christina Alice, b. May 30, 1849 ; d. Nov. 10, 1858.
(248)   Emma Jane, b. Feb. 19, 1853 ; d. Aug. 19, 1853.

V. (235a) Reuben C. Tilden married December 5, 1844, Christina S. Shafter of Thetford, Vt.

CHILD.

VI.   (249)   Reuben Appleton, b. Dec. 16, 1845.

VI. (249) Rueben Tilden married August 31, 1867, Julia A. Fullington of Hanover, N. H.

CHILDREN.

VII.   (250)   Alice Margann, b. —— ; d. ——.
              Clinton Appleton, b. Aug. 14, 1875.

He married (second time) Emma Ames of Norwich, Vt.

V. (236a) Timothy Tilden married April 4, 1849, Marcia A. Harrington of Norwich, Vt.

CHILD.

VI.   (251)   Byron, b. July 6, 1851.

ARMSTRONG.

V. (237) Fannie F. Tilden married April 30, 1840, Samuel A. Armstrong of Norwich, Vt.

CHILDREN.

VI. (252) John W., b. March 10, 1841.
(253) Olive, b. 1842 ; d. 1842.
(254) Henry Allen, b. July 17, 1845 ; d. Oct. 1, 1862.
(255) Olive Ann, b. Aug. 22, 1850.
(256) Fannie, b. May 15, 1859.
(257) Verona T., b. Sept. 5, 1869.
(258) Samuel Jerome, b. March 11, 1861.

VI. (252) John W. Armstrong married November 28, 1861, Philomela H. Boardman of Norwich, Vt.

CHILDREN.

VII. (259) Bethana C. B., b. March 3, 1863.
(260) Henry Allen, b. Sept. 6, 1864.
(261) George Myron, b. Feb. 3, 1866.
(262) John William, b. June 30, 1867.
(263) Mary B., b. Feb. 10, 1869.
(264) Harriette B., b. Feb. 10, 1872 ; d. March 6, 1872.

CUSHMAN.

V. (238) Sophia Tilden married December 5, 1839, Oliver Cushman of Norwich, Vt.

CHILDREN.

VI. Timothy Dexter, b. June 20, 1842.
Elvira Sophia, b. March 24, 1847.
Wesley Oliver, b. Sept. 5, 1850.
Charles Henry, b. Oct. 12, 1857 ; d. Dec. 1, 1895.
Thomas Allerton, b. Sept. 26, 1862.

WATERMAN.

VI. Elvira S. Cushman married January 22, 1867, Truman W. Waterman of Norwich, Vt.

CHILDREN.

VII. Leslie Herbert, b. Nov. 17, 1875.
Ella Cushman, b. Oct. 20, 1883.

CUSHMAN.

VI. Wesley Oliver Cushman married May 18, 1876, Annie Heap of Manchester, N. H.

CHILDREN.

VII. Harry Norris, b. Nov. 17, 1880 ; d. April 17, 1884.
Oliver Wesley, b. April 28, 1886.

VI. Charles Henry Cushman married September 18, 1882, Addie Iola Taft of Manchester, N. H.
VI. Thomas Allerton Cushman married November 24, 1887, Luna J. Blaisdell of Hanover, N. H. She died September 9, 1896.

CHILDREN.

VII. Waldo Emerson, b. Sept. 4, 1888.
Harold Allerton, b. May 28, 1892.
Luna Evelyn, b. Aug. 15, 1896.

LEWIS.

V. (239) Lois L. Tilden married December 7, 1843, Edward Morton Lewis of Norwich, Vt.

CHILDREN.

VI. (265) Lyman, b. Nov. 20, 1844.
(266) George Edward, b. Aug. 10, 1846.
(267) Ransom Tilden, b. Aug. 7, 1848.
(268) Frank Styles, b. Oct. 27, 1852 ; d. March 1, 1854.
Mary Louise, b. Feb. 16, 1857.

5

VI. (265) Lyman Lewis married April 19, 1869, Clara L. Worth.

CHILDREN.

VII. Grace Alberta, b. May 1873, at Norwich, Vt.
Edward Morton, b. Aug. 17, 1879, at Chicago, Ill.; d. at Chicago, Ill., Feb. 9, 1880.

He married (second time) at Chicago, Ill., July 28, 1885, Ann Louise Hoyle.

CHILD.

VII. Katie Louise, b. Jan., 1887.

VI. (266) George Edward Lewis married March 8, 1875, Anna Henrietta Dudley.

CHILDREN.

VII. Frank Edward, b. May 23, 1879.
Charles Arthur, b. July 31, 1883.

VI. (267) Ransom T. Lewis married December 25, 1873, Mattie Ann Howard.

CHILDREN.

VII. Leon Ransom, b. April 29, 1875.
Edward Howard, b. Sept. 25, 1881.
Ernest Eugene, b. Nov. 6, 1886.
Ula Mattie, b. July 6, 1888.

STRONG.

V. (240) Verona Tilden married May 1, 1845, Roger Strong of Thetford, Vt.

CHILDREN.

VI. (269) Charles, b. Dec. 21, 1847.
     (270) Samuel, b. Aug. 30, 1854.
     (271) Allen, b. Dec. 27, 1862.

JOHNSON.

V. (242) Ruth Tilden married March 20, 1849, Jason O. Johnson of Norwich, Vt.

CHILDREN.

VI. (272) Franklin, b. June 22, 1850.
     (273) Millard Wayne, b. June 4, 1852.
   · (274) Marquis De Lafayette, b. Dec. 12, 1854.
     (275) Ruth Louisa, b. April 2, 1866.

JOHNSON.

V. (245) Jane L. Tilden married June 3, 1856, Anthony Wayne Johnson, brother of Jason O. Johnson.

CHILDREN.

VI. (276) Clyma Jane, b. Sept. 23, 1858.
     (277) Hattie, b. July 10, 1860 ; d. June 21, 1863.
     (278) Katie, b. July 10, 1860 ; d. March 20, 1863.
     (279) Lucian Wayne, b. Nov. 15, 1866.

ROOT.

VI. (276) Clyma Jane Johnson married Clarence Root of Norwich, Vt.

CHILD.

VII. One daughter.

JOHNSON.

VI. (279) Lucian W. Johnson married Abbie Waterman of Norwich, Vt.

GOVE.

V. (243) Theta Tilden married July 15, 1852, Albigence P. Gove of Norwich, Vt.

CHILD,

VI. (280) Reuben Albigence, b. Oct. 6, 1853.

Mr. Gove died in April, 1855.

TAYLOR.

V. (246) Mary Sophia Tilden married January 1, 1868, Josiah Taylor of Thetford, Vt.

CHILD.

VI. (281) F. Jeduthan, b. June 6, 1870.

DANFORTH.

VI. (255) Olive Ann Armstrong married September 23, 1868, William A. Danforth of Norwich, Vt.

CHILDREN.

VII. (282) Fannie V., b. Aug. 22, 1869 ; d. Feb. 10, 1870.
(283) Alice, b. Dec. 20, 1871.

KNAPP.

VI. (257) Verona T. Armstrong married March 2, 1892, Arthur S. Knapp of Norwich, Vt.

TILDEN.

IV. (222) Joel Tilden married Sarah Bowen of Lebanon, N. H. Their children were three daughters and one son. Names unknown.

LORD.

III. (9) David Lord married, about 1782, Hannah Hanks, who some years before had ridden on horseback with her father from Mansfield, Conn., to Norwich, Vt. On her first coming to town David Lord was the first man she saw, but then only as a stranger and ferryman across the Connecticut river.

CHILDREN.

IV. (284) Asa, b. Oct. 14, 1783 ; d. March 16, 1861.
(285) David, b. about 1785.
(286) Zalmon, b. about 1787.
(287) Richard, b. Aug. 5, 1788 ; d. April 30, 1863.
(288) Ira, b. about 1791.
(289) Roxana, b. about 1793 ; d. Jan. 22, 1844.
(290) Cynthia, b. about 1795 or 1797 ; d. Feb. 22, 1846.
(291) David Gibson, b. about 1795 or 1797 ; d. Feb. 6, 1869.

IV. (284) Asa Lord married, in 1804, Ruth Howe of Thetford, Vt. She was born in 1782 or 1783 ; died August 20, 1826.

CHILDREN.

V. (292) Ira, b. Feb., 1805 ; d. April 6, 1883.
(293) Lyman, b. 1806 ; d. Sept. 22, 1829.
(294) Abigail, b. Sept., 1809 ; d. Oct., 1865.
(295) Lucia Maria, b. March, 1812 ; d. Nov. 24, 1880.
(296) Gideon, b. Sept., 1814 ; d. April 9, 1898.

(297)   Amasa Converse, b. Dec. 5, 1816; d. Feb. 25, 1901.

(298)   Laura, b. June, 1819; d. Dec. 4, 1879.

(299)   Asa Mills, b. Feb. 28, 1823.

Asa Lord married (second time), 1830, Amelia Root of Norwich, Vt.

CHILDREN.

V.   (300)   Frances Amelia, b. Jan. 31, 1831.

(301)   Abel, b. Nov., 1832; d. Sept. 25, 1834.

(302)   Emma A., b. July 1, 1835; d. June 28, 1853.

(303)   M. Ellen, b. Sept. 18, 1838; d. May 3, 1896.

(304)   William, b. Aug. 26, 1840.

(305)   Henry, b. Aug. 26, 1840; d. May 29, 1842.

(306)   Persis, b. Sept. 26, 1844.

Mr. Lord had his home on the farm his father bought, and in the house his father built, in Norwich, Vt. He was a deacon of the First Congregational Church of Norwich, from 1820, till it was disbanded in 1850 or 1851; he was often called to act in church councils, being looked upon as a man of most excellent judgment, and as having great insight into matters; he was also frequently chosen to transact business for the town.

V.   (292)   Ira Lord married April 17, 1834, Sarah Senter of Thetford, Vt. She was born September 9, 1808; died ———

Mr. Ira Lord had his home for a term of years on a farm about a mile south of Thetford Hill, but he afterwards bought a farm just south of North Thetford, where he died, and where his son John G. L. now has his home.

CHILDREN.

VI. (307) Ira Wilder, b. July 25, 1837; d. at Chicago, Ill., Jan. 13, 1862.
(308) Henrietta Maria, b. June 14, 1842; d. date unknown.
(309) Marietta Sarah, b. June 14, 1842.
(310) John Gilson Lyman, b. Oct. 2, 1848.

VI. (309) Marietta S. Lord married December 4, 1857. Name not given.

VI. (310) John G. L. Lord married September 6, 1871, Charlotte Belden Webster of Thetford, Vt.

CHILDREN.

VII. (311) Sarah Senter, b. Sept. 19, 1872.
(312) Fred Ira, b. Nov. 26, 1879.
(313) Mildred C., b. April 16, 1885.

BOND.

VII. (311) Sarah S. Lord married, in the autumn of 1894, Mr. Burns Bond of Fairlee, Vt.

CUMMINGS.

V. (294) Abigail Lord married December, 1849, William Cummings of Norwich, Vt.

SENTER.

V. (295) Lucia Maria Lord married April 30, 1840, Isaac Tarbell Senter of Thetford, Vt.

CHILDREN.

VI. (314) Lewis Burns, b. June 14, 1841; d. Feb. 28, 1864. Died of the measles in the army hospital, being sergeant in Co. G, Tenth Regt. Vermont Volunteers.

(315) Charles Converse, b. July, 1844.

(316) Lucia Ann, b. Jan., 1851.

VI. (315) Charles C. Senter married June 8, 1886, Emeline Fifield of West Lebanon, N. H.

TENNEY.

VI. (316) Lucia Ann Senter married, date unknown, a Mr. Tenney of North Hanover, N. H. They had their home in South Norwich, Vt.

LORD.

V. (296) Gideon Lord married March 18, 1872, Bellicent Clough of Woodsville, N. H. They have an adopted son. Mr. Lord has his home on Norwich Plain.

V. (297) Amasa Converse Lord pursued his preparatory course of study at Thetford Academy, and entered Dartmouth College in 1839, and graduated in course in 1843 ; he then entered Lane Theological Seminary at Walnut Hills, Cincinnati, Ohio, and graduated in 1846, and entered on the work of the ministry ; he was employed for several years by the American Home Missionary Society in Illinois, but finding this work too severe for him he bought a farm in Somonauk, Ill., where he made a home for himself and accumulated a snug little fortune.

Mr. A. C. Lord married November 8, 1848, Sarah Leonard Gould; she was the daughter of Rev. Nahum Gould, then in the employ of the American Home Missionary Society, as a missionary in Illinois; she was born November 18, 1828, in McDonough, N. Y.

CHILDREN.

VI. (317) Edward Nahum, b. Sept. 27, 1049, in Sharon, Ill.; d. March 23, 1890, at North Ontario, Cal.
(318) William Wilberforce, b. July 3, 1854, at Adams, Ill.
(319) Mary Elizabeth, b. Dec. 25, 1860; d. April 16, 1863.
(320) Abigail, b. March 22, 1863; d. Aug. 16, 1863.
(321) Theodore Hartzell, b. July 9, 1866.
These three younger all born in Adams, La Salle county, Ill.

VI. (317) Edward Nahum Lord married August 26, 1880, Amelia Maria Breeze, at Victor, De Kalb county, Ill. Mr. E. N. Lord was a graduate of Knox College, Illinois, and had been a minister of the gospel for years in different places.

VI. (318) William Wilberforce Lord married March 13, 1884, in Adams, La Salle county, Ill., Mrs. Grace Elisabeth Child of Norwich, Vt.

CHILDREN.

VII. (322) Jessie Margarette, b. May 6, 1886.
Ruth (Helen), b. Nov. 8, 1892.

Mr. W. W. Lord after living for a term of years in Somonauk, Ill., bought a farm in Goldfield, Ia., and removed to it in March, 1895; here he died September 23, 1896, from the effect of a kick on the forehead by a horse in his stable. His widow, Mrs. Grace E. Lord, married (third time) November 4, 1897, at Somonauk, Ill., Mr. John C. Fowler of East Richmond, Va., where her home now is.

VI. (321) Theodore H. Lord married March 9, 1892, Ella Sweet.

CHILD.

VII. Lucy Pearl, b. April 8, 1893.

V. (298) Laura Lord married May 9, 1839, Jonathan Smith Lord of Norwich, Vt. (See No. 159.)

V. (299) Asa Mills Lord married May, 1856, Olivia Ann Seaver of Norwich, Vt.

CHILDREN.

VI. (323) Joseph Irwin, b. March 21, 1857.
    (324) Charles, b. Dec., 1863; d. Oct., 1868.
    (325) Alice Seaver, b. Jan. 5, 1868.

Mr. Asa M. Lord has his home in Norwich, Vt., south of Union Village.

CLOGSTONE.

VI. (325) Alice S. Lord married, date unknown, Mr. Clogstone of Norwich, Vt. They have one son.

V. (304) William Lord married September 7, 1863, Harriet E. Mack of Union Village, Vt.

CHILDREN.

VI. (326) Etta Amelia, b. July 19, 1864.
(327) Alice Louisa, b. Oct. 8, 1873.

Mr. William Lord has his home in Woodsville, N. H.

BAILEY.

VI. (326) Etta Amelia Lord married June 27, 1884, Rev. Charles R. Bailey of Haverhill, N. H. His present home is North Oxford, Mass.

CHILDREN.

VII. (328) William Cullen, b. June 27, 1886.
(329) A son, b. Feb. 27, 1889.

COLBURN.

V. (306) Persis Lord married July 25, 1868, Myron S. Colburn, of Union Village, Vt.

CHILDREN.

VI. (340) Emma Frances, b. June 18, 1874.
(341) Mary Ethel, b. May 17, 1880.
(342) Carrie Emerson, b. Nov. 14, 1882.
(343) Annie Christabelle, b. Sept. 7, 1885.

LORD.

IV. (286) Zalmon Lord married Phila Snow, Mr. Z. Lord went into the United States Army during the war of 1812, and died at Plattsburg, N. Y.

CHILDREN.

V. (344) Zalmon, b. ——.
   (345) Richard, b. ——; d. 188-.
   (346) Hannah, b. ——; d. 1868 or 1869.
   (347) Charles, b. ——.

V. (344) Zalmon Lord married at Lowell, Mass., and resides at or near there; he had two or three children.

V. (345) Richard Lord lived and died unmarried in Norwich, Vt.

NYE.

V. (346) Hannah Lord married Samuel H. Nye of Norwich, Vt.; painter by trade.

CHILDREN.

VI. Samuel, b. Nov. 2, 1832.
     Albert R., b. March 16, 1834.
     Charles D., b. Nov. 14, 1836.
     Mary M., b. ——; d. ——.
     Irena, b. ——; d. ——.
     James Wilbur.

LORD.

IV. (287) Richard Lord married Polly Cadwell, of Thetford, Vt., probably. She was born April 10, 1793; died 1871.

CHILDREN.

V. (348) Mary, b. Nov. 14, 1813.
   (349) Edna, b. March 29, 1816.
   (350) Sophia, b. Sept. 1, 1818.

(351) Achsa, b. July 4, 1820.
(352) Azuba, b. April 27, 1826.
(353) Eleanor, b. Jan. 7, 1823.
(354) Jerusha, b. Dec. 5, 1830.
(355) Lucy, b. April 20, 1834.
And two other children who died in infancy.

V. (348) Mary Lord married Walden F. Cross of
Hanover, N. H., in 1834. They have had ten children,
seven of whom are now living. (1897.)
Mr. Richard Lord had his home for years on the
banks of the Connecticut river in Norwich, Vt., south
of the mouth of the Pompanoosuc, and near the old
ferry. In 1835 he removed to Jackson, Mich., with all
his family—seven daughters—except his eldest one,
and there he lived and died.

HOWE.

IV. (289) Roxana Lord married January 11,
1816, Hugh P. Howe of Thetford, Vt. He died May
21, 1884.

CHILDREN.

V. (356) David Lord, b. Feb. 3, 1817.
(357) Solon, b. 1819 ; d. in infancy.
(358) Solon C., b. Oct. 21, 1821 ; d. Aug. 5, 1897.
(359) Cynthia M., b. Sept. 1, 1823 ; d. Sept. 22, 1899.
(360) Maria, b. ——; d. May 14, 1902.
(361) Sarah Abigail, b. Jan. 17, 1825; lives in
Woodstock, Vt.
(362) Hugh Mills, b. May 21, 1828; d. March, 1868.
(363) Ruth Ann, b. 1830.

(364) Cornelia Frances, b. Dec. 22, 1832 ; d. April 29, 1888.

(365) Nelson, b. Sept. 13, 1837 ; d. Nov. 24, 1883.

(366) Laura Ann, b. Aug. 25, 1839 ; d. ——.

(367) Henry E., b. Dec. 30, 1844 ; d. Jan., 1883.

Mr. Hugh P. Howe for a term of years had his home in Thetford, Vt., and then with all his family removed to Woodstock, Vt.

V. (356) David L. Howe married March 12, 1837, Elizabeth Silver of Norwich, Vt. ; she died in Northfield, Vt., December 28, 1858.

CHILD.

VI. Frances, b. in Chelsea, Vt., April 26, 1859.

Married (second time) December 13, 1865, Mrs. Mary A. Haisington. Mr. Howe was in the army of the Rebellion three years as a soldier, and was discharged at the close of the war.

POWERS.

VI. Frances Howe married Lyman Powers, a conductor on the Central Vermont Railroad, who was killed at White River Junction by being run over by an engine.

HOWE.

V. (358) Solon C. Howe married Eunice Benson, at Lowell, Mass., in 1847.

CHILDREN.

VI. Charles and Ella F.

In the construction of the Passumpsic railroad from Windsor to St. Johnsbury, Vt., Mr. Howe had a very important part, taking large jobs in grading the road-bed. After the completion of this road, he removed to northern New Hampshire, near the line of Canada, where he lived till his death.

RICHMOND.

V. (359) Cynthia Howe married June 13, 1854, Clifton Richmond, who was born July 4, 1828; died June 21, 1896.

CHILDREN.

VI. Mary L., b. June 26, 1856 ; d. Feb. 19, 1876.
Fred C., b. May 27, 1860.
They live in Pomfret, Vt. P. O., Woodstock, Vt.

HOWE.

V. (362) Hugh Mills Howe married 1852, Mrs. Aliss Hayhurst of Worthington, Va.

CHILD.

VI. Alice Cornelia, b. March 7, 1854. She is married and lives in Boston, Mass. (Mrs. Alice Whitcomb.)

Married (second time), 1861, Mrs. Ann Crawford of Ohio.

CHILD.

VI. Stella, b. 1862.

He was conductor on the cars in Indiana, and was killed in 1868 by the explosion of the engine on the train he was conducting.

BRADLEY.

V. (364) Cornelia F. Howe married 1853, Charles Bradley.

CHILDREN.

VI. Elizabeth, Carrie, Georgiana, Edward, and Elna. Part of these live in St. Albans, or Rutland, Vt.

STAPLES.

V. (366) Laura A. Howe married, 1867, Cullen Staples. He died July 18, 1886.

CHILDREN.

VI. Frederic, b. May 28, 1868.
Lucian, b. Aug. 25, 1870.
William, b. May 30, 1872.
These sons live in Woodstock, Vt.

HOWE.

V. (367) Henry E. Howe married, when and whom unknown. He was in the employ of a railroad company in Indiana, and was killed by an engine in the yard of the company, at Indianapolis, January, 1883. He was a soldier in the army of the Rebellion.

IV. (290) Cynthia Lord married about 1827, Reed P. Howe. He was a brother of Hugh P. Howe, and both were brothers of Ruth Howe, wife of Asa Lord. Mr. Howe was born in Henniker, N. H., August 19, 1793; died in Thetford, Vt., March 31, 1892, being nearly 99 years old—98 years, 7 months and 12 days.

CHILDREN.

V. (368) Jesse Reed, b. 1828 ; d. May 28, 1831.
(369) Henry Clay, b. Nov. 30, 1830 ; d. in childhood.
(370) Arabella J., b. Nov., 1831 ; d. Dec. 26, 1883.
(371) Hannah Elizabeth, b. April 30, 1834 ; d. Feb. 26, 1873. Not married.
(372) Charles Carroll, b. Nov. 30, 1836 ; unmarried.
(373) Sarah Roxana, b. March 25, 1839.

Mr. Reed P. Howe had his home at Thetford Center, Vt., and later near Thetford Hill.

PAYSON.

V. (370) Arabella J. Howe married November 8, 1870; married (second time) Albert Payson of Foxboro, Mass. No children. Mr. Payson died February 23, 1873.

PALMER.

V. (373) Sarah Roxana Howe married July 2, 1859, J. Foster Palmer. Mr. Palmer died in the war of the Rebellion November, 1861.

CHILD.

VI. Harry B., b. date not known.

LORD.

IV. (291) David Gibson Lord married Mary Ann Wilson of Norwich, Vt. She died February 6, 1869.

CHILDREN.

V. (374) David Wilson, b. 1821; d. Sept., 1844.
(375) Sarah Cummings, b. 1823; d. April 8, 1900.
(376) Jane M., b. 1826; d. Feb. 9, 1899.
(377) Newton Alphonso, b. Nov., 1829; d. June 13, 1898.
(378) Elizabeth, b. 1835.
(379) William Henry, b. 1832; drowned in 1838.
(380) Nancy Pierce, b. 1844; d. April 5, 1862.

DEWEY.

V. (375) Sarah C. Lord married June 15, 1842, Amos Dewey of Hanover, N. H., where is their home.

CHILDREN.

VI. (381) Ella R., b. April 25, 1851.
(382) Grace S. b. March 30, 1853.
(383) Charles Gibson, b. June 5, 1860.

VI. (381) Ella R. Dewey married November 20, 1878, Lewis P. Merrill; they live at Etna (village), Hanover, N. H.

VI. (383) Charles G. Dewey graduated A. B. at Dartmouth College in 1881; in 1885 graduated M. D. in the medical department; and from 1895 was assistant superintendent in the Boston City Hospital four years; he now is a practicing physician at 539 Talbot Ave., Ashmont, Mass. He married March 21, 1899, at Lowell, Mass., Alice L. Manson.

CHILD.

VII. Robert Manson, b. Aug. 23, 1900.

MORSE.

V. (376) Jane M. Lord married Edward Morse of West Fairlee, Vt.

CHILD.

VI. (384) Leonard Bassett.

Leonard B. Morse married and has one child, P. O., South Fairlee, Vt.

LORD.

V. (377) Newton A. Lord married Violet Burgess. They have six children. They lived for a while in Lowell, Mass., then in West Fairlee, Vt., and then removed to Grand Isle, Neb.

PROPER.

V. (378) Elizabeth Lord married Horace M. Proper of Franklin, Vt.

CHILDREN.

VI. (385) Jenny, b. ——.
(386) William Gibson.
Another son and daughter died in infancy.

COBURN.

V. (380) Nancy P. Lord married Royal Cutter Coburn.

CHILD.

VI. (387) William G., lives at Bradford, Vt.

LORD.

III. (12) Joseph Lord married January 1, 1788, Mary Hovey of Lyme, N. H. Her father then lived on Grant's island, in Connecticut river, between Lyme and Thetford, Vt. Mr. Lord had his home in Windsor, Vt., for fourteen years, where ten of his thirteen children were born, and then he lived for a term of years in Norwich, on the Pompanoosuc river, somewhere between Union Village and its mouth. In 1806 he decided to emigrate West; he was then in reduced circumstances, so that in purchasing horses and the large covered wagon for the journey he needed the assistance of his relatives; with the help of his nephew, Asa Lord, he started from Charlestown, N. H., and arrived with his family at Cincinnati, Ohio, October 29; on a farm in the neighborhood he settled with all his children. January 6, 1807, he wrote his brother Jonathan of Norwich, Vt., describing his journey and safe arrival.

CHILDREN.

IV. (388) Lucinda, b. 1789; d. Germantown, Ohio, about 1849.
(389) Pamelia, b. April 21, 1791; d. 1810.
(390) Mary, b. April 21, 1791; d. Wabash, Ind., Aug. 15, 1871.
(391) Joseph Tilden, b. April 14, 1793; d. Cooper, Sangamon Co., Ill., July 24, 1845.
(392) John Paine, b. Oct. 30, 1795; d. 1829.
(393) Alice, b. Oct. 30, 1795; d. Nov. 12, 1842.

(394)   Ruth, b. July 25, 1797 ; d. Evansport, Ohio,
        Oct. 31, 1873 or 1874.
(395)   David, b. Jan. 5, 1800 ; d. unmarried.
(396)   Jonathan, b. Jan. 5, 1800 ; d. Newton, Ohio,
        1850.
(397)   Abiel Hovey, b. April 26, 1802 ; d. Bellefon-
        taine, Ohio, May 15, 1890.
(398)   Rhoda, b. 1804 ; d. Germantown, Ohio, 1808.
(399)   Rebecca, b. Jan. 10, 1807 ; d. Hamilton, Ohio,
        Sept. 15, 1829.
(400)   Abigail, b. April 30, 1811 ; d. near Cincinnati,
        Ohio.

FRAZER.

IV. (388) Lucinda Lord married, 1839, William
Frazer of Green county, Ohio, a native of Scotland,
Eng. They lived in Germantown, Ohio.

CRARY.

IV. (389) Pamelia Lord married about 1808,
John Crary, a native of Vermont.

CHILD.

V.   (401)   Phebe, b. 1809 or 1810 ; she died young.

BRADBURY.

IV. (390) Mary Lord married Josiah Bradbury,
1809.

CHILDREN.

V.   (402)   Susanna, b. Oct. 11, 1809 ; d. Aug. 16, 1835.
     (403)   Joseph, b. Dec. 3, 1810 ; d. June 3, 1811.
     (404)   John Lord, b. Sept. 29, 1812 ; d. Oct. 8, 1866.
     (405)   James, b. Dec. 9, 1814 ; d. March 13, 1848.

(406)   Lucinda Araminta, b. Aug. 26, 1816 ; d. ——.
(407)   Mary, b. Jan. 11, 1819 ; d. Dec. 27, 1875.
(408)   David, b. May 10, 1821 ; d. ——,
(409)   Sarah Jane, b. Feb. 17, 1825 ; d. ——.
(410)   Rebecca Ann, b. Sept. 29, 1827 ; d. ——.
(411)   Abner Marsh, b. Dec. 29, 1830 ; d. ——.
(412)   Prosper Nichols, b. June 22, 1832 ; d. ——.
(413)   Samuel Harrison, b. March 20, 1834 ; d. Sept. 22, 1849.
(414)   Abiel Hovey Lord, b. Feb. 19, 1837 ; d. March 26, 1862.

Mr. Bradbury's home was in Wabash county, Ind.

V.   (404)   Rev. John Lord Bradbury married, name unknown, and died leaving three daughters.

CHILDREN.

VI.   (415)   Isabella.
       (416)   Matilda.
       (417)   Virginia.

ROXELL.

VI.   (417)   Virginia Bradbury married a Mr. Roxell, who had his home in Marion, Grant county, Ind.

BRADBURY.

V.   (405)   James Bradbury married, name unknown.

CHILD.

VI.   (418)   Leona, b. —— ; only child.

FULTON.

V. (406) Lucinda A. Bradbury married Rev. Joseph Fulton, who resides near Somerset, Ind.

KELLEY.

V. (407) Mary Bradbury married Edward Kelley; she died leaving two daughters.

CHILDREN.

VI. (419) Ida Jane.
(420) Martha Araminta.

BRADBURY.

V. (408) David Bradbury married a Miss Crabtree, who died of cholera within a fortnight after marriage. Married (second time), name unknown, and place of his residence unknown.

DUZAN.

V. (409) Sarah Jane Bradbury married Peter Edwin Duzan of Dora, Wabash county, Ind. The mother of this Mr. Duzan was the daughter of Williams, the famous scout of General Washington in Revolutionary days.

CHILD.

VI. (421) Emma Frances, b. May 26, 1858; d. Oct. 24, 1876.

BRADBURY.

V. (412) Prosper N. Bradbury married, name unknown.

CHILDREN.

VI. (422) Albert Rudolph.
(423) Blanche.

LORD.

IV. (391) Joseph T. Lord married April 16, 1811, Maria Ross of Urbana, Ohio. Their home is Cooper, Sangamon county, Ill.

IV. (392) John Paine Lord married (first) Mary Bogart of Ohio, November 19, 1819. She died 1828, Cincinnati, Ohio. He married (second) Velinda Oswell.

BERRYMAN.

IV. (393) Alice Lord married, 1815, James Berryman. She died about 1819, Cincinnati, Ohio.

CHILDREN.

V. (424) Louisa Amanda, b. Oct. 17, 1816.
(425) William Edward, b. Sept. 3, 1818.

V. (424) Louisa A. Berryman married (first) October 18, 1834, Dolby Merritt; he died July 28, 1849. Married (second) Dennis Donaway.

V. (425) William E. Berryman married November 30, 1840, Sarah Jane Leslie, born in Albany, N. Y.

CHILDREN.

VI. (426) Mary Louisa, b. Oct. 6, 1846.
(427) Katherine Cook, b. Jan. 29, 1848.
(428) Ada Gertrude, b. July 19, 1852.
(429) Hattie Fillian, b. Oct. 16, 1865.

FITHIAN.

VI. (426) Mary L. Berryman married August 16, 1866, William C. Fithian of Cincinnati, Ohio. He has his home in Emporia, Kan. They have four children.

GLENNY.

VI. (427) Katherine C. Berryman married December 30, 1869, Samuel Horace Glenny of Cincinnati, Ohio. They live in St. Louis, Mo.

CHILDREN.

VII. (430) Alice Belle, b. July 19, 1872.
  (431) Arthur Horace, b. Dec. 11, 1873.

ADAMS.

VI. (428) Ada G. Berryman married June 4, 1871, Crawford C. Adams of Cincinnati, Ohio. They live in Washington, D. C., and have three children.

HARRISON.

IV. (393) Alice Lord Berryman married (second) October 19, 1822, Samuel Harrison, who (1877) was living in Elenor, Clermont county, Ohio.

CHILDREN.

V. (432) Margaret, b. July 30, 1823.
 (433) Lucinda Alice, b. March 5, 1825.
 (434) Oliver Kelley, b. May 27, 1827; d. Nov. 13, 1856.

GEORGE.

V. (432) Margaret Harrison married December 26, 1840, Charles George of Cincinnati, Ohio; of whom, and family, no further knowledge.

INGRAHAM.

V. (433) Lucinda A. Harrison married October 14, 1841, Henry Ingraham of Cincinnati, Ohio; he died July 20, 1848; married (second) James Ritter of No. 445 North street, Cincinnati, Ohio. Family unknown.

BENNETT.

IV. (394) Ruth Lord married (first) 1815, Aaron Bennett, born 1773 near Richmond, Va., and died November, 1817, at St. Louis, Mo.

CHILD.

V. (435) Aaron, b. Dec. 14, 1815; died Cincinnati, Ohio.

Mr. Bennett had his home in Evansport, Ohio. He married (second time) July 2, 1841, Rebecca Shaefer of Springfield, Ohio.

CHILDREN.

VI. (436) William Thomas, b. May 13, 1842.
   (437) Orlando, b. May 13, 1845.
   (438) Valentine, b. Dec. 14, 1846; d. July 14, 1847.
   (439) Mary Alice, b. Sept. 14, 1849.
   (440) Susan May, b. March 17, 1851.
   (441) Caroline, b. Feb. 28, 1853.

(442) Adaline, b. Feb. 25, 1855 ; d. Aug., 1861.
(443) Fanny, b. May 1, 1856 ; d. April 26, 1857.
(444) Louisa Adele, b. Feb. 15, 1858.
(445) Clara Bell, b. Dec. 10, 1860.

VI. (436) William T. Bennett married January 1, 1864, Mary Spangler of Defiance, Ohio.

VI. (437) Orlando Bennett married September 21, 1869, Margaret Ann Buck of Bryan, Ohio. Mr. Bennett's home was or is Evansport, Ohio.

CHILDREN.

VII. (446) Minnie Belle, b. Sept. 10, 1870.
     (447) Van Orlo, b. April 9, 1872 ; d. May 4, 1876.

KINTHIGH.

VI. (439) Mary Alice Bennett married October 4, 1867, Thomas Harbaugh Kinthigh of Defiance, Ohio.

CHILDREN.

VII. (448) John Edward, b. Feb. 14, 1872.
     (449) Jane Belle, b. April 21, 1873.
     (450) James Bennett, b. April 12, 1874.
     (451) Mary Idena, b. April 2, 1875.
     (452) Fanny Ethel, b. July 2, 1877.

VI. (441) Caroline Bennett married, July 6, 1872, Harrison T. Kinthigh ; residence, Hicksville, Ohio.

CHILDREN.

VII. (453) Maggie Belle, b. June 20, 1873.
     (454) Forrest, b. Sept. 8, 1874.
     (455) Mary Wilnetta, b. May 25, 1877.

LEWIS.

IV. (394) Ruth Lord Bennett married (second time), 1819, John Lewis of Cincinnati, Ohio. He was a native of Scotland, and died in New Orleans, La.

CHILDREN.

V. (456) Mary Jane, b. May 23, 1820 ; d. Sept. 4, 1858.
(457) Charles Demeter, b. July 14, 1837.
(458) Caroline Cordelia, b. Dec. 16, 1839.
(459) William Malcolm, b. Oct. 27, 1841.
(460) Rebecca Alice, b. Feb. 29, 1843.
(461) Aaron Bennett, b. June 5, 1846.
(462) Edward, b. Aug. 29, 1848 ; died young.
(463) Mary Jane, b. Aug. 28, 1849 ; died young.
(464) Moses, b. Sept. 7, 1851.
(465) Emma Jane, b. Nov. 7, 1855.
(466) Flora Fredonia, b. Aug. 7, 1857.

REPLOGLE.

V. (456) Mary Jane Lewis married February 10, 1834, Frederick George Replogle of Germantown, Ohio. He had his residence in Evansport, Ohio.

CHILD.

VI. (467) Louisa Edith, b. April 13, 1835.

SWARTZEL.

VI. (467) Louisa E. Replogle married, 1853, Jeremiah Swartzel of Germantown, Ohio.

CHILDREN.

VII. (468) John Coleman.
(469) Emma Jane.
(470) Charles Daniel.

(471) Mary Lewis.
(472) William James.
(473) Frank Lewis.
(474) Oliver Jeremiah.
(475) Andrew Patrick.
(476) Peter Robert.
(477) Edward Lord.

LEWIS.

V. (457) Charles D. Lewis married October 27, 1861, Alice Maria Sprague of Springfield, Ohio.

CHILDREN.

VI. (478) Mary Alice.
(479) Charles Elmer.
(480) John Stout.
(481) George Horace.
(482) Bertha Harriet.
(483) Grace Edna.

Mr. Lewis' residence, Evansport, O.

DAWSON.

V. (458) Caroline C. Lewis married Zedekiah Dawson. His residence, Marysville, Ind.

LEWIS.

V. (459) William M. Lewis married Lucy Austin. His residence, Evansport, Ohio.

EVANS.

V. (460) Rebecca A. Lewis married October 16, 1866, John Freeman Evans. Residence, Bryan, Ohio.

LEWIS.

V. (461) Aaron B. Lewis married May 12, 1872, Mary Ellen Caulkins of Williams Center, Ohio. His residence, Bryan, Ohio.

CHILDREN.

VI. (484) Leona, b. July 2, 1873.
(485) Willard Clyde, b. Oct. 26, 1875.

BUTTS.

V. (466) Flora F. Lewis married Julian J. Butts. His residence, Saginaw, Mich.

FRAZER.

IV. (394) Ruth Lord Lewis married (third time) Rev. William Frazer, the former husband of her eldest sister, Lucinda Lord.

KEMP.

IV. (394) Ruth Lord Frazer married (fourth time) the Rev. John Kemp.

STOUT.

IV. (394) Ruth Lord Kemp married (fifth time) Rev. John Stout, a preacher of some note.

LORD.

IV. (391) Joseph Tilden Lord married Maria Ross of Urbana, Ohio, April 16, 1811.

CHILDREN.

V. (486) Mary Ann, b. Jan. 12, 1813.
(487) Minerva Maria, b. Oct. 27, 1818.
(488) Philander Augustus, b. Oct. 3, 1819.
(489) William Nelson, b. Feb. 13, 1821.
(490) Edwin Harvey, b. Sept. 4, 1822.
(491) Elizabeth Winnifred, b. Sept. 7, 1825.
(492) Joseph Edwin, b. Feb. 27, 1831.
(493) James Newton, b. March 22, 1837.
(494) Pamelia Alice, b. May 1, 1840 ; d. March, 1866.

McELROY.

V. (486) Mary Ann Lord married February 9, 1837, William McElroy ; he died in Springfield, Ill.

CHILDREN.

VI. (495) Joseph Robert, b, 1838.
(496) Eliza Jane, b. April 10, 1839.
(497) William Henry, b. 1842.
(498) Ann Maria, b. 1844.

HOONDORF.

V. (486) Mary Ann (Lord) McElroy married November 28, 1844, John Francis Hoondorf of Springfield, Ill.

CHILDREN.

VI. (499) Ann Sophia, b. Sept. 4, 1845.
(500) Mary Elizabeth, b. Aug. 14, 1848.
(501) Sabilla Jane, b. June 17, 1852.
(502) John Francis, b. Oct. 13, 1857.
(503) Charles Newton, b. March 29, 1860.

He was born in Amsterdam, Holland; died in Champaign county, Ill.

TIERY.

V. (487) Minerva M. Lord married May 21, 1840, Henry Tiery of Sangamon county, Ill. He was a farmer there.

VI. (504) Mary Elizabeth, b. March 16, 1841.
  (505) Sarah Katherine, b. Aug. 4, 1843.
  (506) Ann Maria, b. March 6, 1846.
  (507) Joseph Francis, b. Dec. 27, 1848.
  (508) Alice Jane, b. July 4, 1851.
  (509) Lewis Edwin, b. July 12, 1854.
  (510) Eliza Mendora, b. March 2, 1857.
  (511) John Henry, b. Nov. 13, 1859.

LORD.

V. (488) Philander Augustus Lord married November 28, 1850, Margaret Ann Oliver of Mechanicsburg, Ill. He has a farm at Mount Pulaski, Ill.

CHILDREN.

VI. (513) Joseph Edwin, b. May 10, 1852; d. Jan. 28, 1869.
  (514) William Alanson, b. June 8, 1857.
  (515) John Henry, b. May 27, 1860.
  (516) Lundy Augustus, b. Oct. 5, 1862.
  (517) Alice Florence, b. July 17, 1865.

V. (489) William Nelson Lord married, 1851, Sarah Jane Neer of Sangamon county, Ill.

CHILDREN.

VI. (518) Mary Ann, b. Jan. 10, 1852.
    (519) James Edwin, b. Oct. 13, 1853.
    (520) William Harvey, b. March 6, 1856.
    (521) Emma Frances, b. Nov. 12, 1857.
    (522) Sarah Annette, b. Dec. 28, 1861.
    (523) Ida Mary, b. July 18, 1863.
    (524) Charles Hervey, b. July 6, 1865.
    (525) Nellie Grant, b. March 1, 1869.
    (526) Nora Elizabeth, b. Nov. 16, 1870.
    (527) Minnie Florence, b. June 16, 1875.

V. (490) Edwin Harvey Lord married August 6, 1861, Mrs. Mary Elizabeth Ramsdall of Yamhill county, Oregon. He died April 21, 1902.

CHILDREN.

VI. (528) Annette Sophia, b. July 18, 1862.
    (529) Charles Edwin, b. May 29, 1864.
    (530) Richard Hinton, b. April 6, 1866.
    (531) Ionia, b. Feb. 25, 1868.
    (532) Roswell Tilden, b. April 1, 1870.
    (533) Elnora Edith, b. June 26, 1873.
    (534) Alena Agnes, b. Dec. 4, 1875.

[Exchange.]
EDWIN H. LORD DEAD.

END OF A VETERAN PIONEER.

CROSSED PLAINS IN 1850, DUG OUT AND SUNK FORTUNES IN MINING CAMPS—WAS BORN IN URBANA.

Edwin Harvey Lord died from heart failure at the home of his daughter, Mrs. Claude Johnson, in Chelan,

7

April 21, in the eightieth year of his age. He was born in Urbana, Ohio, September 3, 1822. In 1850 he crossed the plains and since that time has covered the coast from Lower California, Mexico, to Caribou, B. C., on horseback, says the *Leader*.

In the ups and downs of a prospector's life he dug out and sunk great fortunes in the mining camps, first in Josephine Gulch, Ore., and later in the gold fields of California and between whiles followed his trade of bricklaying and plastering in Sacramento. As a packer and trader in 1852–'58 he had few equals on this coast. He brought horses from Lower California and sold them to the settlers and in 1858 took a pack train of goods from The Dalles, Ore., to Caribou, B. C., where he sold it for $1.00 per lumping pound of flour, bacon, sugar, etc. He traveled across a trackless country with chart and compass, and on this trip he camped at Moses lake with Chief Moses and his Indians, at a time when they were more apt to plunder than to protect a pack train.

He started the first store in Canyon City, Ore., in 1860. In 1861 he married Mrs. Mary E. Ramsdall at the home of her father, James Brown, in Yamhill, Ore. Since this time he has been a rancher. Now starting an orchard in the Walla Walla or Yakima valleys, and again raising cattle, horses or sheep at Tillamook or Heppner, Ore.

He was the organizer and first president of the company which built the Konewock ditch, since utilized by the Sunnyside Canal Company, in Yakima county.— *Spokesman-Review, Spokane, Wash.*

Ross.

V. (491) Elizabeth Winnifred Lord married Andrew Ross of Rochester, Sangamon county, Ill. Mr. Ross has a family of five children.

Lord.

V. (492) Joseph Edwin Lord married March 2, 1862, Mrs. Elizabeth Ellen Miller of Fort Scott, Kan. Mr. Lord was killed by the fall of a mill at Wyandotte, Kan., January, 1865.

CHILDREN.

VI. (535) Joseph Edwin, b. Nov. 27, 1862, at "Twin Springs," Linn Co., Kan.
(536) Louisa Alice, b. May 21, 1864, at Del Norte, Rio Grande Co., Col.

His widow married William Stitt of Del Norte, Col.

V. (493) James Newton Lord married Elizabeth Rhinehart. He is a stock raiser in Oregon, living there (as is supposed) in 1879.

McFarland.

V. (494) Pamelia Alice Lord married March, 1866, William McFarland of Taylorsville, Ill. They have children, but number unknown.

Lord.

IV. (392) John Paine Lord married November 9, 1819, Mary Bogart of some place in Ohio, though his home seems to have been at Cincinnati, Ohio.

CHILDREN.

V. (537) Joseph Oliver, b. Nov. 5, 1820; d. 1837. (?) He is said to have been drowned in the Ohio river, off the steamer "Roselle."

(538) Jane Elizabeth, b. Nov. 5, 1822.

(539) Mary Ann, b. May 12, 1825.

IV. (392) John Paine Lord married (second time) about 1832, Velinda Oswell.

CHILDREN.

V. (540) Cynthia Ann, b. 1834; d. young.

(541) Jonathan, b. in Danville, Ill., 1836; d. 1856.

(542) Richard, b. 1839; d. 1851 in Rockport, Ill.

(543) Ellen, b. 1841, in Springfield, Ill.

(544) Child, b. 1843; d. in Springfield, Ill., in 1846.

REEDER.

V. (538) Jane Elizabeth Lord married July 10, 1837, Jacob Franklin Reeder of Ottawa, Ill.

CHILDREN.

VI. (545) Joseph Oliver, b. Dec. 15, 1838.

(546) Juliette, b. Jan. 3, 1840.

(547) Cynthia Ann, b. Nov. 14, 1841.

(548) Oscar, b. Oct. 9, 1843.

(549) William C., b. April 30, 1846.

(550) Mary A., b. May 23, 1848.

(551) Nathaniel M., b. July, 1857.

(552) Charles, b. March 30, 1865.

VI. (545) Joseph Oliver Reeder married February 13, 1858, Julia Cochran. They have two children.

Shaefer.

VI. (546) Juliette Reeder married February 25, 1858, Benjamin Shaefer. They have four children.

Loonberger.

VI.. (547) Cynthia Ann Reeder married October 10, 1864, John Loonberger. They have five children.

Reeder.

VI. (548) Oscar Reeder married April 16, 1873, Sophia Wadman of Seneca, Ill.

VI. (549) William C. Reeder married February 16, 1871, Dorcas McFadden. They have two children.

Quaife.

VI. (550) Mary A. Reeder married April 22, 1871, George Quaife. They have four children.

Duzan.

V. (539) Mary Ann Lord married December 25, 1842, Peter Edwin Duzan of Lockport, Ind.

CHILDREN.

VI. (553) John William, b. Dec. 15, 1843; d. Jan. 28, 1879.
(554) Sarah Jane, b. Dec. 4, 1845.
(555) Mary Catherine, b. Feb. 4, 1848.
(556) Henry Sandham, b. Oct. 27, 1850.
(557) Oliver Edwin, b. Dec. 22, 1852.
(558) Elizabeth Ellen, b. March 22, 1856; d. March 8, 1889.

VI. (553) John William Duzan married March 14, 1866, Mary Ellen Dick. He was a soldier in the Union army.

CHILDREN.

VII. (775) Edwin Jerome, b. Oct. 16, 1867; d. Oct. 23, 1870.
(776) Lulu Belle, b. Dec. 19, 1869.
(777) Charles Merritt, b. May 8, 1874.

FRAZEE.

VI. (558) Elizabeth Ellen Duzan married 1876, Isaac Frazee; two years after their marriage, at Springfield, Ill., they removed to Bates county, Mo.

LORD.

IV. (396) Jonathan Lord married January 22, 1824, Sarah Stewart of Newton, Ohio.

CHILDREN.

V. (559) David Alexander, b. Oct. 24, 1824; d. Aug. 28, 1825.
(560) Mary Jane, b. Jan. 5, 1826; d. in the South.
(561) Sarah Ann, b. April 6, 1828.
(562) Nancy, b. Dec. 14, 1830; d. 1832.
(563) Julia Ann, b. Feb. 8, 1832; d. 1832.
(564) Eliza, b. Feb. 8, 1832; d. 1847.

IV. (396) Jonathan Lord married (second time) December 25, 1834, Mrs. Margaret Jones.

CHILDREN.

V. (565) Emeline, b. Sept. 25, 1835.
(566) Julia Ann, b. Jan. 23, 1838.
(567) Almira Jane, b. July 11, 1844.

WEBSTER.

V. (561) Sarah Ann Lord married John Webster of Harpers Station, Ross county, Ohio. They had children, but how many not known.

FRAZER.

V. (565) Emeline Lord married November 29, 1860, Nathaniel Frazer of Tobasco, Ohio.

CHILDREN.

VI. (568) Cora, b. March 12, 1862.
(569) Benton, b. March 18, 1864; d. Dec. 26, 1864.
(570) Emma, b. July 9, 1866.
(571) William, b. July 28, 1868.

WITHAM.

V. (566) Julia Ann Lord married July 26, 1853, . William Witham of Withamsville, Ohio.

CHILDREN.

VI. (572) Louis, b. Aug. 11, 1854.
(573) Nathaniel Freemont, b. July 4, 1856.
(574) Owen Allen, b. May 8, 1866.

VI. (573) Nathaniel Freemont Witham married Mary Elizabeth Archer, December 25, 1877.

HANKS.

V. (567) Almira Jane Lord married June 5, 1872, James Hanks of Newtown, Ohio. One adopted son.

LORD.

IV. (397) Abiel Hovey Lord, M. D., married May 27, 1824, Letitia McCloud of Bellefontaine, Ohio. Mr. Lord had located, May, 1823, at Bellefontaine, Logan county, Ohio, as a physician, and was thrice elected treasurer of Logan county.

CHILDREN.

V. (575) Maria Eliza, b. April 23, 1825.
(576) Lucinda, b. July 2, 1828.
(577) Minerva, b. April 15, 1830.
(578) Richard Sprigg Canby, b. Oct. 26, 1832 ; d. Oct. 15, 1866.

MORE.

V. (575) Maria Eliza Lord married May 18, 1841, Lorenzo Gavit More, a farmer of Bellefontaine, Ohio. He was born in Licking county, March 13, 1818 ; died July 4, 1896.

CHILDREN.

VI. (579) Robert Abiel, b. March 17, 1842.
(580) Caroline Lucinda, b. May 23, 1844.
(581) Joseph Lord, b. June 11, 1847 ; d. June 4, 1888.
(582) Letitia McCloud, b. Aug. 10, 1849.
(583) Sally Gavit, b. Dec. 4, 1851 ; d. Dec. 18, 1876.
(584) Richard Lord, b. May 4, 1854.
(585) Minnie Malvina, b. Nov. 4, 1865.
William, b. Feb. 10, 1857 ; d. March 9, 1857.
Paul, b. Dec. 24, 1859 ; d. April 11, 1865.
Lorenzo Gavit, Jr., b. Feb. 27, 1864 ; d. March 17, 1865.

PARISH.

VI. (580) Caroline Lucinda More married February 18, 1874, William Andrew Parish of Licking county, Ohio.

MORE.

VI. (581) Joseph Lord More married September 2, Jennie Carmonie of Miamo county, Ohio.

CHILDREN.

VII. Letitia, Jessie, and Maria Louise.

NEER.

VII. Letitia More married Shurman Neer of De Groff county, Ohio.

CHILD.

VIII. Gertrude, b. 1900.

CROUSE.

VI. (582) Letitia McCloud More married February 22, 1893, George W. Crouse of Fort Wayne, Ind.

WRIGHT.

V. (576) Lucinda Lord married March 31, 1846, Thomas Lee Wright, M. D.

CHILDREN.

VI. (586) Abiel Lord, b. April 3, 1847; he was also a physician of Bellefontaine, Ohio.
(587) Thomas Huntington, b. April 30, 1849. He became a counsellor at law.

(586)   Abiel Lord Wright married March 4, 1869, Clara Gregg of Bellefontaine.

HACKENGER.

V.   (577)   Minerva Lord married August 6, 1862, her cousin, George Morton Hackenger, a farmer.

CHILDREN.

VI.   (588)   Richard Lord, b. March 29, 1864.
   (589)   James Clarence, b. April 12, 1869.

LORD.

V.   (578)   Col. Richard Sprigg Canby Lord married July 4, 1863, Mary Angelina Wright of Hamilton county, Ohio.

CHILDREN.

VI.   (590)   Richard Stanton, b. April 9, 1864, in Hamilton Co., Ohio.
   (591)   Edith Sheridan, b. May 20, 1865; d. Sept. 8, 1865.

Col. Lord died of pneumonia at Bellefontaine, Ohio, and his widow afterwards married James K. Goodwin, Esq., of Peoria, Ill.

Col. Lord graduated at West Point in 1856; he served as Brevet Major, First United States Cavalry, during the War of the Rebellion, participated in many of the hard fought battles of the Potomac, was wounded in the battle of Gettysburg, and for gallant and meritorious conduct at the battle of "Five Forks" was raised to the rank of *Colonel.* Major Lord was high minded and most honorable in all his instincts, and his record as a soldier was most honorable. He participated in numerous engagements, and in all of them he shone as a brave and skilful officer. His conduct at " Five Forks" was the theme of public commendation in all the newspapers of the land, called forth the special and personal approval of Major General Sheridan, and was the occasion of his receiving brevet promotion.

His career through life was highly creditable, and his decease, while yet in the prime of life, was regarded as a public loss, and was universally lamented by sincere and loving friends.

The above is taken from Cleveland Genealogy.

HASKINSON.

IV. (399) Rebecca Lord married September 20, 1827, John Haskinson of Portsmouth, Ohio.

CHILD.

V. (591) A daughter, b. Sept. 15, 1829 ; died soon.

HACKENGER.

IV. (400) Abigail Lord married January 16, 1828, Protus Hackenger of Cincinnati, Ohio.

CHILDREN.

V. (592) Mary Alice, b. Oct. 16, 1830.
(593) Josephine, b. March 16, 1833 ; d. May 2, 1851.
(594) George Morton, b. June 20, 1835.

(595) William Henry, b. Nov. 18, 1838; d. July 14, 1841.
(596) Agnes, b. Jan. 6, 1840.
(597) Mary Magdalene, b. March 17, 1843.
(598) William Henry, b. March 17, 1845.
(599) James Ritter, b. Aug. 20, 1846.
(600) Joseph Lord, b. Nov. 15, 1849.
(601) Charles Francis, b. July 20, 1853.
(602) Sarah Jane, b. July 3, 1856.

HOFFMAN.

V. (592) Mary Alice Hackenger married September 12, 1850, Philip Hoffman of Cincinnati, Ohio.

CHILDREN.

VI. (603) Philip, b. Aug. 27, 1850; d. Nov. 4, 1850.
(604) Charles, b. Sept. 9, 1851.
(605) Philip, b. Jan. 14, 1854; d. Sept. 11, 1875.
(606) Francis, b. Feb. 24, 1856; d. March 17, 1860.
(607) Alice, b. Jan. 16, 1858.
(608) William, b. Feb. 5, 1860, in Jackson, Ohio.
(609) Laura, b. March 15, 1862, in Newport, Ky.
(610) Agnes, b. Feb. 1, 1865, in Williams, Ohio.
(611) John, b. Aug. 3, 1867, in Aberdeen, Ohio.

HACKENGER.

V. (594) George Morton Hackenger married August 6, 1862, Minerva Lord, his cousin. [See No. (577)]. He married (second time) December 20, 1877, Ada Eda Shirwall.

FROMMEGER.

V. (596) Agnes Hackenger married May 1, 1860, Francis Garrett Frommeger of Cincinnati, Ohio.

CHILDREN.

VI. (612) Mary Frances, b. Sept. 1, 1862.
(613) Agnes Philamona, b. May 18, 1864.
(614) Josephine, b. April 2, 1866; d. Oct. 12, 1867.
(615) John Francis Elied, b. Oct. 2, 1868.
(616) Albert Eugene, b. May 30, 1870.
(617) Vincent Frederick, b. Feb. 22, 1873; d. Nov. 2, 1873.
(618) Arthur Ferdinand, b. March 29, 1875.

EVNST.

V. (597) Mary Magdalene Hackenger married September 26, 1865, Joseph Evnst of St. Genevieve, Mo.

CHILDREN.

VI. (619) Francis Joseph Adam, b. Sept. 23, 1866.
(620) John Edward, b. Nov. 5, 1868.
(621) William Anthony, b. Nov. 26, 1870.
(622) Mary Alice, b. May 3, 1872.
(623) Florence, b. Nov. 6, 1874.
(624) Henry, b. Jan. 18, 1877.

HACKENGER.

V. (598) William Henry Hackenger married January 24, 1868, Elizabeth Christina Cook. He is a farmer at Sedansville, Ohio.

CHILDREN.

VI. (625) Louisa May, b. Oct. 17, 1868.
(626) William Henry, b. June 30, 1872; d. Aug. 31, 1872.
(627) James Ritter, b. Jan. 10, 1874.
(628) John Cook, b. Dec. 4, 1875.

(This account of Ichabod Lord and family is placed here last in order of place and numbers because the records and information were received after all the others had been written and arranged.)

III. (11) Ichabod Lord, b. Bolton, Conn., April 7, 1763. (This is the date given in his family Bible.) d. Shalersville, Portage Co., Ohio, May 16, 1852.

His father removed from Bolton, Conn., to Hanover, N. H., in the spring of 1766, probably living in different parts of that town till the fall of 1773, when he removed to Norwich, Vt. He lived and died on the banks of the Ompompanoosuc river, and was buried in the old cemetery on the bluff down near its mouth. The remains of himself and wife are still there. The boyhood of Ichabod, their son, was spent in these two towns.

In 1785, probably, he married Rebecca (Abels?) of Bolton, Conn. She was born in Bolton, Conn., April 18, 1763; died in Shalersville, Ohio, July 18, 1826.

After his marriage he lived somewhere in Norwich, Vt., for a term of years, his two eldest children being born there. Before 1790, or during that year, he removed to Brookfield, Vt., living on the second branch of the White river, not a long distance from East Randolph village, and up the stream on the west side of the road.

Somewhere about 1806 he removed to Middletown, Rutland county, Vt., and lived there some ten years; but in 1816 he removed to Shalersville, Ohio, where he died at the age of eighty-nine years. (In 1852.)

CHILDREN.

IV. (629) Amarilla, b. Norwich, Vt., March 31, 1786 ; d. in Alliance, Ohio, about 1880, being nearly 94 years old.

(630) Horatio, b. Norwich, Vt., Nov. 22, 1787 ; d. Martinsburg, Ill., 1859. (One account says he died 1856.)

(631) Leantha, b. Brookfield, Vt., Feb. 4, 1790 ; d. in Missouri, date unknown.

(632) Sarah, b. Brookfield, Vt., June 20, 1792 ; d. about 1848.

(633) Philena, b. Brookfield, Vt., Nov. 1, 1794; d. Oct. 28, 1828.

(634) Alanson, b. Brookfield, Vt., Nov. 25, 1796 ; d. April 24, 1828.

(635) Ichabod, b. Brookfield, Vt., April 10, 1799 ; d. Shalersville, Ohio, Aug. 3, 1826.

(636) Reuben C., b. Brookfield, Vt., June 22, 1802 ; d. in Winston, Mo., about 1887.

(637) Elmeria (or Almira), b. Brookfield, Vt., Dec. 21, 1804 ; d. in Port Byron, Ill., date unknown.

(638) David, b. Middletown, Vt., Sept. 30, 1808 ; d. Trenton, Mo., Feb. 4, 1893.

WALDO, OR WALDOW.

IV. (629) Amarilla Lord while living in Vermont, married a Mr. Waldo, time and place unknown. When her father's family removed to Ohio, they seem to have gone too, for she died in Alliance, O. They had four children. (Three or four.)

LORD.

IV. (630) Horatio Lord married in Portage county, Ohio, date unknown, Nancy Davidson.

CHILDREN, ALL BORN IN PORTAGE COUNTY, OHIO.

V.　(639)　Albert, d. aged 14.
　　　　　An infant child.
　(640)　Lucinda, b. (when?)
　(641)　Philander, b. 1822; d. April 20, 1896.
　(642)　Lucretia, b. —.
　(643)　Louisa, b. —.
　(644)　Ichabod, b. —.
　(645)　Mary, b. about 1836; d. 1887.
　(646)　Curtis, b. Oct. 16, 1838.

Horatio Lord lived in Portage county, Ohio, till 1836, when he removed first to some part of Iowa and then over into Illinois, living and dying at Martinsburg, Pike county, where most of his children live, or were living recently.

BELL.

V.　(645)　Mary Lord married a Mr. Bell, date not given.　They had their home for many years in Ripley county, Missouri.　(May be his home is there still with a daughter.)

CHILDREN.

VI.　(647)　Solomon, b. ——; his residence is in Jamestown, Ark.
　(648)　Electa, b. ——.

LORD.

V.　(646)　Curtis Lord married March 24, 1864, Margaret D. Troutman.　She was born September 1, 1847.

CHILDREN.

VI. (649) Eliza, b. Oct. 31, 1865 ; d. Nov. 15, 1867.
(650) Lucretia, b. June 3, 1867.
(651) Sarah, b. Oct. 7, 1868.
(652) Albert, b. Oct. 13, 1870.
(653) Emily, b. Sept. 12, 1872.
(654) John W., b. Dec. 15, 1874 ; d. Sept. 8, 1875.
(655) Franklin, b. Dec. 10, 1877.
(656) Curtis, b. March 10, 1880.
(657) Clara, b. Feb. 10, 1882.
(658) Mina, b. June 18, 1884.
(659) Artie May, b. Feb. 13, 1889.

SMITH.

VI. (650) Lucretia Lord married John Smith, date and place unknown. They have two children.

ROBINSON.

IV. (632) Sarah Lord married a Robinson, date and place unknown.

CHILDREN.

V. (660) Lucas (or Lewis). He lived at one time at Chardon.
(661) Andrew, he died in youth.

PELLIS.

IV. (633) Philena Lord married a Pellis, date unknown. Their home may have been at Middleburg, Ohio, where she died; date unknown.

8

LORD.

IV. (634) Alanson Lord married about 1820, Freedom Loomis. She was born June 2, 1801; died October 11, 1874.

CHILD.

V. (649a) Jasper, b. Shalersville, Ohio, Aug. 5, 1822; d. June 6, 1879.

Mr. Alanson Lord and his son were both noted carpenters and builders all over Portage county; in addition they had the management of their farm, the homestead of his father.

V. (649a) Jasper Lord married September 10, 1858, Mary Ann Smith; she was born at Mt. Blanchard, Hancock county, Ohio, October 6, 1839.

CHILDREN.

VI. (650a) Freedom Luette, b. Shalersville, Ohio, Jan. 12, 1851; d. Topeka, Kan., Sept., 1891.

(651a) William L., b. Drummond Springs, Mich., Dec. 29, 1860.

RANDLEBUSH.

VI. (650a) Freedom Luette Lord married E. H. Randlebush, and they had their home in Topeka, Kan. They had two children, names not given.

LORD.

VI. (651a) William L. Lord married August 9, 1880, Helen Moore of Charlestown, Portage county, Ohio.

CHILD.

VII. (652a) Stella, b. Aug. 9, 1882.

Leantha Lord and her two brothers, Reuben C. and David, lived in Portage county, Ohio, till 1873, when they all removed to Missouri.

LORD.

IV. (636) Reuben C. Lord married Julia Risley of Aurora, Ohio; she died at Trenton, Mo. Together they forced a fortune out of an unbroken forest, at Aurora, Ohio.

CHILDREN.

V. (662) Mariah.
   (663) Celestia.
   (664) Augusta.
   (665) Carlos.
   (666) Reuben and his twin brother, who died unnamed.
   (667) Elmer. } twins.
   (668) Elmus. }

This Elmus died before the late war.

   (669) Marion.
   (670) Eugene. } twins.
   (671) Emogene. }
   (672) Emma, died young.

This Eugene Lord lives at Winston, Davis Co., Mo.

BIGELOW.

IV. (637) Almira Lord married Timothy Bigelow, time and place unknown. They removed from Ohio about 1844 to Port Byron, Ill. Living or dead not known.

LORD.

IV. (638) David Lord married February 4, 1831, Susan Smith of Aurora, Portage county, Ohio. She died May 9, 1877.

CHILDREN.

V. (673) Lusette, b. May 12, 1832; d. Nov., 1832.
(674) Zalmon David, b. Oct. 30, 1833; d. drowned in 1863.
(675) Weltha, b. March 30, 1836; d. Aug., 1836.
(676) Evalin Susan, b. March 21, 1838; d. no record.
(677) Henry H., b. March 22, 1841; lives at Trenton, Grundy Co., Mo.
(678) Americus J., b. Jan. 14, 1845; lives in Chicago, Ill.
(679) Evalin, b. Sept. 13, 1849; d. Aug., 1850.
(680) Adella, ——; d. when about 5 years old.
A babe that died unnamed.

Index

BEARD (cont)
  W 40 Elwin A 39
  Joseph W 39 Mary 39
  Mary L 40 Milton E 40
  Oscar F 40 Urania 39
  William F 39-40
BELL, Electa 112 Mary
  112 Mr 112 Solomon
  112
BENNETT, Aaron 90
  Adaline 91 Caroline
  90-91 Clara Bell 91
  Fanny 91 Louisa Adele
  91 Mary 91 Mary Alice
  90-91 Mary Ann 91
  Minnie Belle 91 Mr 90-
  91 Orlando 90-91
  Rebecca 90 Ruth 90
  Ruth Lord 92 Susan
  May 90 Valentine 90
  Van Orlo 91 William T
  91 William Thomas 90
BENSON, Eunice 78
BERRYMAN, Ada G 89
  Ada Gertrude 88 Alice
  88 Alice Lord 89 Hattie
  Fillian 88 James 88
  Katherine C 89
  Katherine Cook 88
  Louisa A 88 Louisa
  Amanda 88 Mary L 89

BERRYMAN (cont)
  Mary Louisa 88 Sarah
  Jane 88 William E 88
  William Edward 88
BIGELOW, Almira 115
  Timothy 115
BILLINGS, Harriet 53
BLAISDELL, Luna J 65
BLISS, David 49 Lucy 49
BOARDMAN, Philomela
  H 64
BOGART, Mary 88 99
BOND, Burns 71 Sarah S
  71
BOWEN, Sarah 69
BRADBURY, Abiel Hovey
  Lord 86 Abner Marsh
  86 Albert Rudolph 88
  Blanche 88 David 86-
  87 Isabella 86 James
  85-86 John Lord 85-86
  Joseph 85 Josiah 85
  Leona 86 Lucinda A 87
  Lucinda Araminta 86
  Mary 85-87 Matilda 86
  Mr 86 Mrs 87 Prosper
  N 87 Prosper Nichols
  86 Rebecca Ann 86
  Samuel Harrison 86
  Sarah Jane 86-87
  Susanna 85 Virginia 86

CLOUD (cont)
52 Joseph H 22
CLOUGH, Bellicent 72
COBURN, Nancy P 83
Royal Cutter 83
William G 83
COCHRAN, Julia 100
COFFIN, Aldee B 45
Ferdinand D S 45 Glen
M 45 Sophronia M 45
COLBURN, Annie
Christabelle 75 Carrie
Emerson 75 Elizabeth
41 Emma Frances 75
Mary Ethel 75 Myron S
75 Persis 75
COOK, Elizabeth
Christina 109
COOPER, Roger 3
COPP, Amanda Rebecca
26 Charles 26 Charles
Franklin 26 Lois 25
Lucy Ann Rosamond
26 Sarah Elizabeth 26
CRABTREE, Miss 87
CRARY, John 85 Pamelia
85 Phebe 85
CRAWFORD, Ann 79
CRIPPEN, Experience 9-
10 Jabez 9 Thomas 9
CROSS, Mary 77 Walden

CROSS (cont)
F 77
CROUSE, George W 105
Letitia Mccloud 105
CUMMINGS, A 62
Abigail 71 Asa 62
William 71
CURTICE, 17 Jonathan 15
Mr 16
CURTIS, Agnes Martha 40
Delia P 40 Fred Mason
40 Mary Bessie 40
Mason B 40 Morna
Ellen 40
CUSHMAN, Addie Iola 65
Annie 65 Charles
Henry 64-65 Elvira S
64 Elvira Sophia 64
Harold Allerton 65
Harry Norris 65 Luna
Evelyn 65 Luna J 65
Oliver 64 Oliver
Wesley 65 Sophia 64
Thomas Allerton 64-65
Timothy Dexter 64
Waldo Emerson 65
Wesley Oliver 64-65
DANFORTH, Alice 68
Fannie V 68 Olive Ann
68 William A 68
DAVIDSON, Nancy 111

DAVIS, Mary W 38
DAWSON, Caroline C 93
  Zedekiah 93
DEWEY, Alice L 82 Amos
  82 Charles G 82
  Charles Gibson 82 Ella
  R 82 Grace S 82 Robert
  Manson 82 Sarah C 82
DICK, Mary Ellen 102
DIMMOCK, Silence 10
DONAWAY, Dennis 88
  Louisa A 88
DUBY, Katie A 30 Walter
  30
DUDLEY, Anna Henrietta
  66
DUTTON, Alice Lyman 55
  Charles S 55 Charles
  Sumner 54 Daniel B 54
  Ella Frances 55 George
  A 55 George Albinus
  54 George Augustus 55
  Harriet Ann 54 Hattie
  E 55 Hattie Elizabeth
  54 Henry Allen 54 John
  54 Lorana 54 Louisa
  Augusta 54 Mabel
  Frances 55 Mary 55
  Mary Lorana 54
DUZAN, Charles Merritt
  102 Edwin Jerome 102

DUZAN (cont)
  Elizabeth Ellen 101-
  102 Emma Frances 87
  Henry Sandham 101
  John William 101-102
  Lulu Belle 102 Mary
  Ann 101 Mary
  Catherine 101 Mary
  Ellen 102 Mr 87 Oliver
  Edwin 101 Peter Edwin
  87 101 Sarah Jane 87
  101
EASTMAN, Etta L 48
  Hattie B 44
ELLIS, Sally 61
EVANS, John Freeman 93
  Rebecca A 93
EVNST, Florence 109
  Francis Joseph Adam
  109 Henry 109 John
  Edward 109 Joseph 109
  Mary Alice 109 Mary
  Magdalene 109
  William Anthony 109
FELLOWS, Deacon 18
FIELD, Bruce F 27 Bruce
  Fluellen 27 Charlotte
  Belle 27 Josephine M
  27 Leona Aldana 27
  Leonora Alberta 27
  Rhoda W 20 26 Simeon

FIELD (cont)
  C 20 26
FIFIELD, Emeline 72
FITHIAN, Mary L 89
  William C 89
FOWLER, Grace E 52 74
  John C 52 74 Mr 52
FRAREY, Sophia 62
FRAZEE, Elizabeth Ellen
  102 Isaac 102
FRAZER, Benton 103
  Cora 103 Emeline 103
  Emma 103 Lucinda 85
  94 Nathaniel 103 Ruth
  Lord 94 William 85 94
  103
FREEMAN, Charles 28
  Clara 28 Edmund 15
  Emma Josephine 28
  Frances 28 Frank 28
  Mabel Augusta 29 Mr
  16 29 Mrs 16 William
  H 28
FROMMEGER, Agnes
  108 Agnes Philamona
  109 Albert Eugene 109
  Arthur Ferdinand 109
  Francis Garrett 108
  John Francis Elied 109
  Josephine 109 Mary
  Frances 109 Vincent

FROMMEGER (cont)
  Frederick 109
FROST, Carlton Shattuck
  47 Etta L 48 J Newton
  47 Katherine Lord 48
  Lucena L 47 Lucena
  Moore 47 Walter
  Eastman 48 Walter L
  48 Walter Lord 47
  Warren S 47
FULLINGTON, Julia A 63
  William 25
FULTON, Joseph 87
  Lucinda A 87
GEORGE, Charles 90
  Margaret 90
GLENNY, Alice Belle 89
  Arthur Horace 89
  Katherine C 89 Samuel
  Horace 89
GODFREY, Henry 31
  Ruth 31
GOODMAN, Sharon 13
GOODSPEED, Mary J 30
GOODWIN, James K 106
  Mary Angelina 106
GOULD, Nahum 73 Sarah
  Leonard 73
GOVE, Albigence P 68 Mr
  68 Reuben Albigence
  68 Theta 68

GREGG, Clara 106
GUILD, Cemira E 43
  Keziah 41 Lenora
  Constance 43 Luther 43
  Marion Edith 43
  Raymond Lord 43
  Warren Locke 43
HACKENGER, Abigail
  107 Ada Eda 108
  Agnes 108 Charles
  Francis 108 Elizabeth
  Christina 109 George
  Morton 106-108 James
  Clarence 106 James
  Ritter 108-109 John
  Cook 109 Joseph Lord
  108 Josephine 107
  Louisa May 109 Mary
  Alice 107-108 Mary
  Magdalene 108-109
  Minerva 106 108
  Protus 107 Richard
  Lord 106 Sarah Jane
  108 William Henry
  108-109
HAISINGTON, Mary A 78
HANKS, Almira Jane 103
  Hannah 69 James 103
HARRINGTON, Marcia A
  63
HARRISON, Alice Lord

HARRISON (cont)
  89 Lucinda A 90
  Lucinda Alice 89
  Margaret 89-90 Oliver
  Kelley 89 Samuel 89
HASKINSON, Daughter
  107 John 107 Rebecca
  107
HASTINGS, Arthur G 29
  Augusta Marion 29 C
  A 29 Carrie Maria 29
  Charles 29 Charles H
  29 Charles Herbert 29
  Clara Augusta 29-30
  Clarence A 29 Clarence
  Aldis 29 Eva M 29
  Frances Marion 29
  Frank Herbert 29
  Gracie Gertrude 29 Mr
  29 Nellie Gertrude 29
  Robert Clark 29
HATCH, 20
HAYHURST, Aliss 79
HEAP, Annie 65
HERRINGTON, Elvira 37
HILL, Ruth 27
HILLS, John 14
HOFFMAN, Agnes 108
  Alice 108 Charles 108
  Francis 108 John 108
  Laura 108 Mary Alice

HOFFMAN (cont)
   108 Philip 108 William
   108
HOOKER, Rev Dr 3
HOONDORF, Ann Sophia
   95 Charles Newton 95
   John Francis 95 Mary
   Ann 95 Mary Elizabeth
   95 Sabilla Jane 95
HOUSE, Col 24
HOVEY, Mary 84
HOWARD, Mary
   Elizabeth 50 Mattie
   Ann 66
HOWE, Alice Cornelia 79
   Aliss 79 Ann 79
   Arabella J 81 Charles
   78 Charles Carroll 81
   Cornelia F 80 Cornelia
   Frances 78 Cynthia 79-
   80 Cynthia M 77 David
   L 78 David Lord 77
   Elizabeth 78 Ella F 78
   Eunice 78 Frances 78
   Hannah Elizabeth 81
   Henry Clay 81 Henry E
   78 80 Hugh Mills 77 79
   Hugh P 77-78 80 Jesse
   Reed 81 Laura A 80
   Laura Ann 78 Maria 77
   Mary A 78 Mr 78-80

HOWE (cont)
   Nelson 78 Reed P 80-
   81 Roxana 77 Ruth 69
   80 Ruth Ann 77 Sarah
   Abigail 77 Sarah
   Roxana 81 Solon 77
   Solon C 77-78 Stella 79
HOYLE, Ann Louise 66
HOYT, Diadema 32 Mr 32
   Wyman 32
HYDE, Eunice 31 Mr 31
INGRAHAM, Henry 90
   Lucinda A 90 Mary 4
   Samuel 4
JENKS, David Elmer 51
   Helen Elizabeth 51
   John E 51 Katherine 51
   Lawrence 51 Leon
   Ralph 51 Lucy E 51
   Margaret Bliss 51
   Marion Walker 51
   Mary Amanda 51
JOHNSON, Abbie 68
   Abbie S 57 Anthony
   Wayne 67 Clyma Jane
   67 Franklin 67 Hattie
   67 Jane L 67 Jason O
   67 Katie 67 Lucian W
   68 Lucian Wayne 67
   Marquis Delafayette 67
   Millard Wayne 67 Mrs

JOHNSON (cont)
  Claude 97 Ruth 67
  Ruth Louisa 67
JONES, Margaret 102
KELLEY, Edward 87 Ida
  Jane 87 Martha
  Araminta 87 Mary 87
KEMP, John 94 Ruth Lord
  94
KENDRICK, James 61
  Ruth 61
KINTHIGH, Caroline 91
  Fanny Ethel 91 Forrest
  91 Harrison T 91 James
  Bennett 91 Jane Belle
  91 John Edward 91
  Maggie Belle 91 Mary
  Alice 91 Mary Idena 91
  Mary Wilnetta 91
  Thomas Harbaugh 91
KNAPP, Arthur S 68
  Verona T 68
LANGLEY, John 39 Mary
  Della 39 Mary E 39
LESLIE, Sarah Jane 88
LEWIS, Aaron B 94 Aaron
  Bennett 92 Alice Maria
  93 Ann Louise 66
  Anna Henrietta 66
  Bertha Harriet 93
  Caroline C 93 Caroline

LEWIS (cont)
  Cordelia 92 Charles
  Arthur 66 Charles D 93
  Charles Demeter 92
  Charles Elmer 93 Clara
  L 66 Edward 92
  Edward Howard 66
  Edward Morton 65-66
  Emma Jane 92 Ernest
  Eugene 66 Flora F 94
  Flora Fredonia 92
  Frank Edward 66
  Frank Styles 65 George
  Edward 65-66 George
  Horace 93 Grace
  Alberta 66 Grace Edna
  93 John 92 John Stout
  93 Katie Louise 66
  Leon Ransom 66 Leona
  94 Lois L 65 Lucy 93
  Lyman 65-66 Mary
  Alice 93 Mary Ellen 94
  Mary Jane 92 Mary
  Louise 65 Mattie Ann
  66 Moses 92 Mr 93
  Ransom T 66 Ransom
  Tilden 65 Rebecca A
  93 Rebecca Alice 92
  Ruth Lord 92 94 Ula
  Mattie 66 Willard
  Clyde 94 William M 93

LEWIS (cont)
William Malcolm 92
LITTLE, Alpa Rosette 52
LOCKE, James 35 Sophia
35
LOMBARD, Darwin 30
Estella H 30 Mary H 30
LONGLY, Emma
Josephine 28
LOOMIS, Freedom 114
LOONBERGER, Cynthia
Ann 101 John 101
LORD, A C 73 Abbie 45
Abbie Sanborn 52 Abel
70 Abiel Hovey 85 104
Abigail 69 71 73 85
107 Achsa 77 Adella
116 Alanson 111 114
Albert 112-113 Alena
Agnes 97 Alice 84 88
Alice Florence 96 Alice
Louisa 75 Alice S 74
Alice Seaver 74 Alicia
Rosette 53 Almira 111
115 Almira Jane 102-
103 Alpa B 49 Alpa R
53 Alpa Rosette 52
Amanda Rebecca 26
Amarilla 111 Amasa
Converse 70 72 Amelia
70 Amelia Maria 73

LORD (cont)
Americus J 116 Amie 3
Amos Jasper 43
Angeline Farnsworth
36 Ann 3 Ann Thane
51 Annette Sophia 97
Artie May 113 Asa 21
51 69-70 80 84 Asa M
74 Asa Mills 70 74
Augusta 115 Augusta
Marion 28-29 Aymie 3
Azuba 77 Bellicent 72
Bernard E 44-45 Bessie
Glee 52 Carlos 115
Caroline 49 Celestia
115 Cemira E 43
Charles 74 76 Charles
C 41 Charles Colburn
44 Charles Edwin 97
Charles G 30 Charles
Hervey 97 Charlotte
Belden 71 Child 100
116 Clara 113 Clarence
44 Clarissa 36 Col 106
Constance A 41
Coraline 41-43 Curtis
112-113 Cynthia 69 80
Cynthia Ann 100 Dan
Guild 42 Daughter 41
46 David 13 20-21 23
69 85 111 115-116

LORD (cont)
David Alexander 102
David B 50 David Bliss
49 David Gibson 69 81
David Wilson 82 Delia
P 40 Dorothy 3-4 E G
34 E N 73 Edith M 41
43 Edith Sheridan 106
Edna 76 Edward
Nahum 73 Edwin G 52 ˙
Edwin Goodell 51
Edwin H 97 Edwin
Harvey 95 97 Eleanor
77 Eleazer W 44
Eleazer Wells 36 Eliza
46 102 113 Eliza
Nelson 52 Elizabeth 41
82-83 99 Elizabeth A
44 Elizabeth Ann
Davis 26 Elizabeth
Ellen 99 Elizabeth
Winnifred 95 99 Ella
74 Ellen 100 Ellen
Sarah 51 Elmer 115
Elmer E 30 Elmeria
111 Elmus 115 Elnora
Edith 97 Emeline 102-
103 Emily 41 113
Emma 115 Emma A 70
Emma C 41 Emma
Frances 97 Emma W

LORD (cont)
44-45 Emogene 115
Estella H 30 Etta
Amelia 75 Ettie M 44
Eugene 115 Eva G 42
Evalin 116 Evalin
Susan 116 Experience
9-10 13 31 Fern E 42
Florence S 41 Frances
28 Frances Amelia 70
Frances L 46 48
Franklin 113 Fred
Ernest 43 Fred Ira 71
Freedom 114 Freedom
Luette 114 Gideon 69
72 Grace E 52 74
Grace Elisabeth 73
Grace Elizabeth 51-52
Hannah 4 9 69 76
Harriet 53 Harriet Ann
50 54 Harriet E 75
Harriet M 46 48 Harvey
Brown 26 Hattie B 44
Hattie M 40 Helen 73
114 Helen Norene 53
Henrietta Maria 71
Henry 70 Henry D 5
Henry H 116 Henry
Holdane 51 Horatio
111-112 Horatio Flagg
50 Ichabod 13 15 25

LORD (cont)
110-112 Ida M 53 Ida
Mary 97 Ionia 97 Ira
69-70 Ira Wilder 71
Isaac 25 Isaac W 20 26
Isaac Walbridge 25
James Edwin 97 James
Harris 46 James
Newton 95 99 James W
42 Jane Elizabeth 100
Jane M 82-83 Jane
Sophronia 43 Jasper 46
49 114 Jennie
Elizabeth 52 Jerusha 77
Jessie Margarette 52 73
John 3-4 6-9 13-14 34
49-50 John F 53 John
Franklin 52 John G L
70-71 John Gilson
Lyman 71 John Henry
96 John L 41 John
Locke 43 John M 53
John Mills 50 53 John
P 41 John Paine 84 88
99-100 John Proctor 36
John W 113 Jonathan 4
6 8 10-11 13-15 17 19-
25 27-28 32-34 84-85
100 102 Jonathan
Smith 49 51 74 Joseph
6 13 16 84 Joseph

LORD (cont)
Edwin 95-96 99 Joseph
Irwin 74 Joseph Oliver
100 Joseph T 88 Joseph
Tilden 84 94 Judah
Albinus 50 Julia 115
Julia Ann 102-103
Justin M 44 Justin
Morrill 41 Katie A 30
Keziah 41 Laura 51 70
74 Leantha 111 115
Lella M 44-45 Lenora
C 41 Lenora Constance
43 Leon Bertie 43
Letitia 104 Lizzie E 42
Lois 25 Louisa 112
Louisa Alice 99 Lucena
L 46-47 Lucia Maria
69 71 Lucinda 46 84-
85 94 104-105 112
Lucius S 52 Lucius
Stebbins 49 Lucretia
112-113 Lucy 26 49 77
Lucy E 51 Lucy
Elizabeth 51 Lucy
Isabel 50 56 Lucy
Lavina 26 Lucy Pearl
74 Lundy Augustus 96
Lusette 116 Luther R
42 Lydia 34 57 Lyman
69 M Ellen 70 Mabel

LORD (cont)
45 Major 107 Margaret
102 Margaret Ann 96
Margaret D 112 Maria
36 88 94 Maria Eliza
104 Mariah 115
Marietta S 71 Marietta
Sarah 71 Marion 115
Marion J 44 Martha N
40 Mary 4 32 34 36 39
76-77 84-85 88 99 112
Mary Angelina 106
Mary Ann 81 95 97
100-101 114 Mary E 44
98 Mary Elizabeth 50
73 97 Mary J 30 Mary
Jane 102 Mary Laurette
49 Mary Lavina 26-27
Mary Lundie 51
Mildred C 71 Mina 113
Minerva 104 106 108
Minerva M 96 Minerva
Maria 95 Minnie E 43
Minnie Florence 97 Mr
5 30 34-35 40 70 72 84
99 104 Mrs Nathaniel
25 Nancy 102 111
Nancy P 83 Nancy
Pierce 82 Nathan 5
Nathaniel 4-5 13 16 20
24-25 Nellie Grant 97

LORD (cont)
Nettie E 42 Newton A
83 Newton Alphonso
82 Nora Elizabeth 97
Olivia Ann 74 Orinda
44 Otis B 5 Pamelia
84-85 Pamelia Alice 95
99 Persis 70 75 Phila
75 Philander 112
Philander Augustus 95-
96 Philena 111 113
Polly 34 76 Porter 34-
36 Porter L 40 Porter
Locke 36 Rachel 34
Ralph C 44 Raymond
Porter 41 Rebecca 25
85 107 110 Reuben 115
Reuben C 111 115
Reuben M 46 48
Reuben Marshall 46
Reuben P 44-45 Rhoda
25 85 Rhoda W 20 26
Rhoda Walbridge 26
Richard 3 69 76-77 100
Richard Hinton 97
Richard Sprigg Canby
104 106 Richard
Stanton 106 Robert 3 5
Roswell Tilden 97
Roxana 69 77 Russell
34 46 Russell 2d 49

LORD (cont)
Russell Carlton 53
Ruth 10-11 13 16 27 58
69 73 85 90 Ruth Helen
52 Sarah 4 8-9 25 46
70 102 111 113 Sarah
Ann 102-103 Sarah
Annette 97 Sarah C 82
Sarah Cummings 82
Sarah E 46-47 Sarah
Ellen 51 Sarah Jane 96
Sarah Leonard 73
Sarah S 71 Sarah
Senter 71 Sophia 35-36
76 Sophronia 44
Sophronia M 44-45
Stella 115 Susan 116
Thankful 26 Theodore
H 74 Theodore Hartzell
73 Theron Arthur 43
Thomas 3-5 9
Tryphena Evaline 26
Velinda 88 100 Violet
83 W W 74 Weltha 116
Wendell E 44 William
3-9 70 75 William
Alanson 96 William
Harvey 97 William
Henry 82 William
Henry A 30 William L
114 William Nelson

LORD (cont)
95-96 William W 52
William Wilberforce 52
73 Wm Henry Aldis 28
Z 75 Zalmon 69 75-76
Zalmon David 116
LYMAN, Ella Frances 55
MACK, Harriet E 75
MANSON, Alice L 82
MARSHALL, Sarah 46
MASON, Lavina 32 Moses
32
MAXUM, Alice 58
MCCLOUD, Letitia 104
MCELROY, Ann Maria 95
Eliza Jane 95 Joseph
Robert 95 Mary Ann 95
William 95 William
Henry 95
MCFADDEN, Dorcas 101
MCFARLAND, Pamelia
Alice 99 William 99
MERRILL, Ella R 82
Lewis P 82
MERRITT, Dolby 88
Louisa A 88
METCALF, Florence
Dutton 56 Frederic
Ernest 56 Hattie E 55
Otis 55 Paul 56
MILLER, Carrie Maria 29

MILLER (cont)
   Elizabeth Ellen 99
MONAHAN, 20
MOORE, Caroline 49
   Helen 114 James 46
   Lucinda 46 Mary 46
MORE, Caroline Lucinda
   104-105 Jennie 105
   Jessie 105 Joseph Lord
   104-105 Letitia 105
   Letitia Mccloud 104-
   105 Lorenzo Gavit 104
   Lorenzo Gavit Jr 104
   Maria Eliza 104 Maria
   Louise 105 Minnie
   Malvina 104 Paul 104
   Richard Lord 104
   Robert Abiel 104 Sally
   Gavit 104 William 104
MORSE, Edward 83
   Ernest L 48 Harriet M
   48 Jane M 83 John M
   48 Leonard B 83
   Leonard Bassett 83
   Lucinda 46 Merritt
   Presby 48 Mr 46
MOSES, Chief 98
NEER, Gertrude 105
   Letitia 105 Sarah Jane
   96 Shurman 105
NELSON, Eva G 42

NYE, Albert R 76 Charles
   D 76 Hannah 76 Irena
   76 James Wilbur 76
   Mary M 76 Samuel 76
   Samuel H 76
OLCOTT, Peter 33
OLIVER, Margaret Ann
   96
OLMSTEAD, Marilla 37
ORDWAY, Lucretia 61
   Sophia 61
OSWELL, Velinda 88 100
PALMER, Harry B 81 J
   Foster 81 Mr 81 Sarah
   Roxana 81
PARISH, Caroline Lucinda
   105 William Andrew
   105
PAYSON, Albert 81
   Arabella J 81 Mr 81
PEABODY, Abbie 45 Mr
   45
PELLIS, 113 Philena 113
PENNOCK, Diadema 31-
   32 Eunice 31
   Experience 31 Lavina
   31-32 Mr 31-32 Ruth
   31 Seraphina 31-32
PIKE, Martha N 40
POWERS, Frances 78
   Lyman 78

PROCTOR, Ann T 57 Ann
Turner 57 John 57
Louisa Lord 57 Lydia
57
PROPER, Elizabeth 83
Horace M 83 Jenny 83
William Gibson 83
QUAIFE, George 101
Mary A 101
RAMSDALL, Mary E 98
Mary Elizabeth 97
RANDLEBUSH, E H 114
Freedom Luette 114
REEDER, Charles 100
Cynthia Ann 100-101
Jacob Franklin 100
Jane Elizabeth 100
Joseph Oliver 100 Julia
100 Juliette 100-101
Mary A 100-101
Nathaniel M 100 Oscar
100-101 Sophia 101
William C 100-101
REPLOGLE, Frederick
George 92 Louisa E 92
Louisa Edith 92 Mary
Jane 92
REYNOLDS, Clara
Augusta 30 Henry H 30
Mr 30 Ruth Marion 30
RHINEHART, Arthur 28

RHINEHART (cont)
Clara 28 Cora 28
Elizabeth 99 John
Edward 28
RICHARDS, Ida M 53
RICHARDSON, David 19-
21
RICHMOND, Clifton 79
Cynthia 79 Fred C 79
Mary L 79
RISLEY, Julia 115
RITTER, James 90
Lucinda A 90
ROBINSON, 113 Andrew
113 Lewis 113 Lucas
113 Sarah 113
RODGERS, John 50
ROGERS, Ambrose 12
Augustine 12 Barnaby
12 Bernard 12
Cassandra 12
Constantine 12 Daniel
12 Edward 12 Elisabeth
12 Eliza 11 Elizabeth
10 Ellen 12 Hannah 11
Hecuba 12 Hester 12
Jabes 10 Joan 12 John
10-12 22-23 33 Joseph
10-11 Mary 11-12 Mr
22 Nathaniel 10-11
Nehemiah 10 Phillip 12

ROGERS (cont)
  Ruth 10-11 13 Samuel
  12 Sarah 11 Silence 10
  Susan 12 Thomas 10-
  13 Varro 12 William
  12
ROOT, Amelia 70
  Clarence 67 Clyma
  Jane 67 Daughter 67
ROSS, Andrew 99
  Elizabeth Winnifred 99
  Maria 88 94 Mr 99
ROXELL, Mr 86 Virginia
  86
RUGGLES, Alpa R 53
  Frederick A 53
SANDERS, Charles 45
  Emma W 45 Louis 45
  Mamie 45
SAWYER, Elmer E 38
  Eveline A 38 Fred A 38
  Zara 38
SEAVER, Olivia Ann 74
SENTER, Charles C 22 72
  Charles Converse 72
  Emeline 72 Isaac
  Tarbell 71 Lewis Burns
  72 Lucia Ann 72 Lucia
  Maria 71 Sarah 70
SHAEFER, Benjamin 101
  Juliette 101 Rebecca 90

SHAFTER, Christina S 63
  John 21-22
SHALER, Mary 4
SHERIDAN, Maj Gen 107
SHIRWALL, Ada Eda 108
SILVER, Elizabeth 78
SKINNER, Thomas 7
SMITH, Edward 32-33
  Franklin 20 25 John
  113 Lorana 54 Lucretia
  113 Mary 32 Mary Ann
  114 Molly 33 Mr 20
  Susan 116 Timothy 20
  32
SNOW, Phila 75
SOUTHWICK, Lawson 27
  Lora Ardena 27 Mary L
  27 Mary Lavina 27
SPANGLER, Mary 91
SPENCER, Lydia E 60
SPRAGUE, Alice Maria
  93 Martha Ann 38
STAPLES, Cullen 80
  Frederic 80 Laura A 80
  Lucian 80 William 80
STEBBINS, Lucy 49
STEWART, Sarah 102
STITT, Elizabeth Ellen 99
  William 99
STOUT, John 94 Ruth
  Lord 94

STOWELL, Elam
Nathaniel 25 Ira 25
Sarah 25
STRONG, Allen 67
Charles 67 Roger 66
Samuel 67 Verona 66
SWARTZEL, Andrew
Patrick 93 Charles
Daniel 92 Edward Lord
93 Emma Jane 92
Frank Lewis 93
Jeremiah 92 John
Coleman 92 Louisa E
92 Mary Lewis 93
Oliver Jeremiah 93
Peter Robert 93
William James 93
SWEET, Ella 74
TAFT, Addie Iola 65
TALCOTT, Benjamin 14
TAYLOR, Clinton 45 F
Jeduthan 68 Florence O
45 Harvey A 45 Jasper
E 45 Josiah 68 Lella M
45 Mary Sophia 68
Noah C 45 Nora E 45
TEELE, Edwin 47 Mr 47
Sarah 47 Sarah E 47
TENNEY, Lucia Ann 72
Mr 72
TIERY, Alice Jane 96 Ann

TIERY (cont)
Maria 96 Eliza
Mendora 96 Henry 96
John Henry 96 Joseph
Francis 96 Lewis
Edwin 96 Mary
Elizabeth 96 Minerva
M 96 Sarah Katherine
96
TILDEN, Alice Margann
63 Betsey 60 Byron 63
Charles 60 Christina
Alice 63 Christina S 63
Clinton Appleton 63
Edna 60 Elisha 59 61
Elvira 63 Emily 60
Emma 63 Emma Jane
63 Emma Josephine 60
Fannie F 63 Fannie
Frarey 62 Finette 61
Jane L 63 67 Joel 60 69
John 59 61 Joseph 59-
60 Julia A 63 Lois L 65
Lois Louisa 62 Lucretia
61 Lydia 59-61 Lydia E
60 Marcia A 63 Mary
60 Mary Elizabeth 60
Mary Sophia 63 68
Melissa 61 Mr 62
Phebe 59 62 Ransom
63 Reuben 63 Reuben

TILDEN (cont)
Appleton 63 Reuben C
63 Reuben
Chamberlain 62 Ruth
59 61 63 67 Sally 61
Sarah 69 Sophia 61-62
64 Thankful 26 Theta
63 68 Timothy 59-60
62-63 Titus 60 Titus W
60 Titus Woodward 60
Verona 62 66
TILLOTSON, Albinus
Lester 37-38 Chester B
36-37 Chester F 37
Clara Ann 38 Cora L
37 Elvira 37 Emma S
37 Eveline 37 Eveline
A 38 George A 38
George L 38 Hattie A
37 Isabel May 38
Lester 36 Lester L 37
Lester M 36 Malvina
37 Malvina M 39
Marilla 37 Martha Ann
38 Martha J 38 Mary E
37 39 Mary W 38
Melora 37 Nellie S 38
Olin L 37 Oramel M
37-38 Oramel O 38
Orlando M 37 Sarah L
38 Son 37 Sophia 36

TILLOTSON (cont)
Sophia Locke 36
William L 38 William
S 38
TOPLIFF, 56 Mary E 56
TOWER, Benjamin 43
Coraline 43 Mr 43
TROUTMAN, Margaret D
112
TWINING, Elizabeth 10
VIRGIN, Mary 60
WADMAN, Sophia 101
WALDO, Amarilla 111 Mr
111
WALLACE, Everean
Bruce Lord 27 John 27
Mary L 27
WASHINGTON, Gen 87
WATERMAN, Abbie 68
Daniel 62 Ella
Cushman 65 Elvira S
64 James 22 50 Leslie
Herbert 65 Phebe 62
Truman W 64
WEBSTER, Charlotte
Belden 71 John 103
Sarah Ann 103
WEST, Alpa B 49 Fannie
48 Frances L 48 Henry
Merritt 48 Mary Burton
48 Mr 32 Presbury 3d

www.ingramcontent.com/pod-product-compliance
Lightning Source LLC
Chambersburg PA
CBHW070251290326
41930CB00041B/2451